The Obedience Code

The Obedience Code

Mindy Sanchez

CONTENTS

1

The Obedience Code
By: Mindy Sanchez

Prologue: The Hidden Code

The rain tapped against the windowpane like a thousand tiny fingers, drumming an insistent rhythm that seemed to echo the pounding of Lila's own heart. She stood in the study, staring at the locked chest in the corner, its dark wood polished to a near-mirror shine. Her father had kept it hidden here, tucked beneath stacks of dusty books and forgotten papers, as if he had known someone—or something—might come looking.

She remembered the day he had died. The official reports said it was an accident—a misstep on the old staircase in the attic—but something in the quiet gravity of the house whispered otherwise. A cold shadow lingered in the corners, a presence she could feel brushing against her skin, unseen yet unmistakable. And now, with the chest in front of her, Lila felt that same chill press against her spine.

The lock was old, heavy, and rusted, but her hands moved with a strange certainty as she fumbled with the key her father had left in a small, folded envelope. The key slid in smoothly, turning with a click that sounded unnaturally loud in the stillness of the room. She lifted the lid, and a faint scent of aged paper and ink reached her, mixing with something metallic, almost electric, that made the hairs on her arms stand on end.

Inside lay a single book, unlike anything she had ever seen. Its cover was black leather, embossed with a symbol that resembled a maze wrapped around an eye. Gold lettering spelled out its title: *The Obedience Code*. The weight of the book was more than physical; it seemed to hum, as if alive, filled with secrets too heavy for ordinary hands.

Lila's fingers traced the spine reverently, hesitantly, before opening it. The pages were filled with strange diagrams, cryptic annotations, and lists of laws that made no sense at first glance. Words like *submission*, *control*, *loyalty*, and *consequence* were repeated, interwoven with patterns and symbols that pulsed with a hidden logic she instinctively felt she could decipher. Each page seemed to thrum with intent, as though it were waiting for her to understand its purpose.

A folded piece of parchment slipped from between the pages, landing at her feet. She picked it up, heart hammering. The handwriting was angular, precise, and chillingly familiar.

"Obey, or you'll be next."

Lila swallowed hard, her pulse spiking. The warning was unmistakable. Someonc had known she would find this book, had known she would read it. Fear prickled at the edges of her mind, sharp and immediate, but curiosity burned brighter. She felt drawn to the knowledge within, as though the book itself had chosen her.

Her father's voice echoed in her memory, calm but urgent: *"Some truths are dangerous, Lila. Some power is not meant for the unprepared."*

Her eyes roamed the pages again, lingering on a diagram that seemed to map the movements of people, their choices, and the consequences of obedience or defiance. Somewhere in the margins, scrawled in a hand she didn't recognize, was a single note: *"They are watching. They always have been."*

Lila's breath caught. Who were *they*? And why had her father left this for her? Questions spiraled through her mind like a storm: Was this a guide? A trap? Or a warning?

She closed the book for a moment, pressing it to her chest, feeling the strange weight of responsibility settle over her shoulders. Something had shifted in the room, or perhaps within her. She was no longer just a teenager mourning a father—she was now the keeper of a dangerous secret, a key to knowledge that could change lives, or end them.

And deep in the shadows of the study, she could have sworn she heard a faint shuffle, the soft click of a door handle, and then silence. Someone—or something—was out there, watching, waiting for her next move.

Lila opened the book again. She had no choice. Curiosity had a price, and she was ready to pay it.

The Obedience Code had begun.

Chapter 1: Lila Finds The Obedience Code

The morning sun barely pierced the gray clouds outside Lila's bedroom window, casting long, pale shadows across the floor. She sat cross-legged on her bed, the black leather book cradled in her hands. *The Obedience Code.* The words seemed to shimmer in the dim light, almost daring her to open it again.

Her mother's voice echoed from downstairs.

"Lila! Are you coming down for breakfast?"

"Coming!" she called, her voice a little too bright. She didn't want anyone to know how unnerved she still felt.

After a quick glance at the book, she slipped it under her pillow and hurried downstairs. Her mother was bustling in the kitchen, the smell of burnt toast and strong coffee filling the air.

"Morning, sweetie," her mother said, smiling but tired-eyed. "I... uh, made extra eggs. Thought you might want some."

Lila forced a smile. "Thanks, Mom." She grabbed a plate and poured herself a cup of orange juice, but her mind was elsewhere. *Who would leave a book like that?*

After breakfast, she excused herself. "I have homework," she said, though she had no intention of doing algebra today. She needed answers.

Back in her room, she carefully lifted the book from under her pillow. The cover felt almost hot to the touch, pulsing slightly under her fingers, as if it recognized her. She opened it to the first page.

The handwriting was immaculate, slanted, and precise, almost surgical in its exactness. Lila read the first line aloud to herself:

"Obedience is the foundation of order. Defiance is the seed of chaos."

A shiver ran down her spine. She wasn't sure why, but the words felt alive, demanding attention.

"Order... chaos..." she whispered, tracing the letters with her finger. "What does this even mean?"

She turned the page. Diagrams sprawled across it—lines connecting circles, triangles, and squares, annotated with strange symbols she didn't understand. In the margins, notes were scribbled in pencil:

"Trust no one completely. Observe first. Obey selectively."

Her heart skipped a beat. *Trust no one... observe first...* The words felt like a warning. But why had her father written this? And for whom?

Lila flipped through more pages, discovering lists of rules, each more unsettling than the last:

"Rule 1: Silence is loyalty.
Rule 2: Compliance is survival.
Rule 3: Questions are dangerous."

Her stomach twisted. "Survival? Dangerous?" she murmured. She could hear her own breath in the quiet room.

A sudden knock at the door made her jump. "Lila, are you okay in there?" Her mother's voice was tinged with concern.

"Yeah, Mom! Just... studying," she called, trying to sound normal.

The knock made Lila more alert. She closed the book quickly, as if hiding it would make the knowledge safer. But the feeling of being watched lingered. She couldn't shake it.

After a few minutes, she reopened the book, her curiosity stronger than her fear. A folded piece of parchment slipped out. Lila picked it up, hands trembling slightly. The paper was fragile, edges yellowed, and the ink sharp and black.

"Obey, or you'll be next."

The words leapt off the page. Lila's eyes widened. "Next? Next for what?"

Her mind raced. *Was it a joke? A warning? Or was it... real?* She remembered the shadows in her father's study, the strange feeling that someone was always watching. Her pulse quickened.

Lila whispered to herself, "I have to know."

She flipped through the book again, skimming more diagrams and annotations. A sketch caught her attention: a room with a single figure in the center, lines radiating outward to smaller figures along the edges. Notes beside it read:

"Influence spreads through obedience. Resistance is detected."

Her breath caught. "Influence spreads... resistance detected... like a network."

Lila sat back, absorbing the enormity of what she held. *Her father didn't just write a book—he left a guide, a warning, a blueprint.* The pieces were slowly forming a picture in her mind: a hidden organization, controlling people through fear, loyalty, and manipulation.

A sudden memory flashed in her mind: the day she had found her father's journal tucked behind his study desk. There had been a note, barely legible: *"Some truths are too dangerous to know... but some must be learned."*

"Why me?" Lila whispered, her voice barely audible. "Why now?"

The book seemed to hum in response, the leather warm against her palms. She traced the embossed symbol on the cover—the maze wrapped around an eye. *They are watching. They always have been.*

The thought sent a chill down her spine. Lila realized she was no longer just reading. She was being called. The words, the diagrams, the rules—they weren't simply information. They were instructions, and she was the intended reader.

Suddenly, the room felt colder, the shadows longer, as if the walls themselves were listening. She hugged the book to her chest, heart racing. She had a choice: close it and pretend it didn't exist, or open it fully and risk everything.

Lila took a deep breath, her fingers trembling but determined. She opened the book once more, and her eyes scanned the pages with a new focus, as if each word contained the key to survival.

A whisper of wind rattled the window, and for a brief second, she thought she saw movement outside. Someone—or something—was watching.

"I'm ready," Lila whispered to the empty room, her voice firm now, not afraid. "Show me the code."

And with that, she began to read.

Chapter 2: Strange Symbols

The morning after discovering *The Obedience Code*, Lila sat cross-legged on her bedroom floor, the black leather book spread open in front of her. Sunlight seeped through the curtains in thin, golden slivers, illuminating the strange symbols scrawled across the first few pages. They looked like a mixture of ancient runes and geometric diagrams, twisting into patterns that made her head spin.

She traced one line with her finger. "What are you trying to tell me?" she whispered, leaning closer. The symbols seemed almost to shift, though she knew it was impossible. Her eyes darted from one figure to another: circles connected by thin lines, triangles with dots at their corners, and swirling spirals that seemed to pulse faintly under the light.

A soft knock at her door made her jump. "Lila? Everything okay?" Her mother's voice was cautious but worried.

"I'm fine! Just... studying," Lila called back, closing the book quickly and tucking it under her pillow.

The moment the door clicked shut, she pulled it back out. She had to understand. Her fingers hovered over a spiral etched with tiny arrows, then traced them slowly. Something clicked in her mind, like a hidden mechanism turning. A line of text at the edge of the page caught her attention:

"Observe first. Obey selectively."

"Observe first... obey selectively..." she repeated, tasting the words. "Is this... instructions? Or warnings?"

Her phone buzzed. A text from her best friend, Mara: *Hey, still coming to lunch?*

Lila hesitated. She wanted to respond casually, but her mind raced with the symbols. Could these shapes be some kind of code? Did her father leave her instructions hidden within them? She typed back, *Yeah, be there in ten,* trying to sound normal.

She returned to the book, flipping to the next page. There were more symbols, but now some seemed familiar, resembling patterns she'd seen in her father's old notebooks. One diagram showed a central figure surrounded by smaller circles, lines connecting them in what looked like a web. Notes scribbled in pencil read:

"Influence spreads through obedience. Resistance is detected."

Lila's breath caught. "Influence spreads... resistance is detected... like a network," she whispered.

Her mind replayed memories of her father's death, the cold shadows in the study, and his cryptic journal entries: *"Some truths are too dangerous... but some must be learned."*

A chill ran down her spine. She closed the book briefly, pressing it to her chest. Was this just a puzzle her father left behind—or a warning?

Then, as if on cue, a shadow moved across her room. Lila froze, heart hammering. She spun around. Nothing. Just the familiar walls, her desk, and the chair her cat had knocked over yesterday.

"Get a grip, Lila," she muttered. "It's just nerves."

But the feeling didn't fade. She knew, somehow, that the symbols weren't just diagrams—they were alive with purpose, waiting for her to decipher them.

Determined, she reopened the book, scanning the next set of pages. Tiny lines of text ran along the margins, almost invisible:

"They are watching. They always have been."

Her fingers trembled as she read it. "Watching... always?"

The thought made her stomach twist. Someone—or something—was monitoring her. But why? And how much had her father known?

A flicker of movement outside the window drew her gaze. A figure, just for a second, disappeared behind the maple tree. Lila's pulse accelerated. *Is it him? Or someone else?*

Her hand hovered over the book again. She felt a pull, irresistible and dangerous, as if the book itself was calling to her. She opened to a new page, filled with symbols she hadn't noticed before: interlocking triangles, spirals, and a strange glyph resembling an eye. Her eyes widened as she realized the glyph repeated throughout the text, always near notes about obedience, loyalty, and consequences.

Lila whispered to herself, voice barely audible: "It's a language... but of what? Power? Control?"

The morning sun shifted, casting a long shadow across the book, and Lila realized she had been staring at it for hours. Hunger, homework, even the world outside her window—none of it mattered. She had crossed a line. The book had her attention, and she couldn't turn back.

For the first time, she spoke aloud, almost as if addressing the shadows themselves:

"I will understand you... even if it kills me."

A cold gust of wind rattled the window, though all the windows were closed. Lila shivered. Somewhere in the quiet house, she thought she heard a soft, deliberate shuffle—like footsteps that weren't meant for her ears.

Her hand clutched the book tighter. She was no longer just a girl searching for answers about her father. She was a participant in something larger, something dangerous, something alive with the promise of secrets she was only beginning to comprehend.

And deep down, she knew: nothing would ever be the same

Chapter 3: Father's Journal

The rain had returned by afternoon, tapping insistently against Lila's window as if echoing her racing thoughts. She sat at her desk, the black leather book laid open, but her eyes kept drifting to the small, dusty notebook she had found beneath her father's study desk the day after his death.

It was ordinary at first glance—a simple leather-bound journal, pages yellowed with age. But the handwriting inside was unmistakable: precise, careful, deliberate. Her father's.

She hesitated before opening it, a lump forming in her throat. Memories of his calm voice, his rare smiles, and the tension in his eyes during his last weeks flooded back. She flipped to a page bookmarked with a torn corner, the ink smudged as though he had pressed too hard in a moment of anxiety.

"If you are reading this, Lila, it means I am gone. Do not mourn too long. Some truths are too dangerous to know, yet too important to leave undiscovered. You must understand what I could not tell you."

Her hands shook. "Dad... what were you involved in?"

She continued reading, each line pulling her deeper into a world she had only glimpsed in fragments:

"The organization watches. It influences everything: schools, jobs, families. Loyalty is manufactured. Obedience is enforced. Those who question are removed... quietly, efficiently."

Lila's eyes widened. "Removed? You mean... people disappear?"

She flipped further, finding a sketch of her father's study, but with a strange overlay of symbols and arrows—lines connecting objects in the room, like the book itself had become a map. Marginal notes read:

"They are closer than you think. Trust must be earned, even with family."

Her heart thudded painfully. She thought of her mother, her little brother, her friends. Were they being monitored? Manipulated? Could she trust anyone?

A sudden creak in the hallway made her jump. “Hello?” Her voice was small, fragile. Silence answered back. She tried to shake it off, but the unease lingered.

Lila whispered to herself, “I have to be careful... for everyone’s sake.”

She turned another page and found an entry in a different hand, slanted, smaller. A warning:

"Obedience is survival. Resist, and you will be tested. Some will betray you... even those you love."

She pressed the journal to her chest, her mind racing. *Resist... tested... betray...* Could her father have known this was coming? Was he already planning for her to continue his work, to protect herself from the organization?

The next page contained a series of numbered instructions, vague but chilling:

1. Observe first.
2. Obey selectively.
3. Trust sparingly.
4. Seek the Code.
5. Prepare for the inevitable.

“I’m supposed to... do all this?” she muttered, tracing each word. “Prepare for the inevitable? What does that even mean?”

Her phone buzzed, startling her. A text from Mara: *Everything okay? You’ve been MIA all morning.*

Lila typed back carefully, *Yeah... just studying.* She couldn’t risk sharing any of this. Not yet. Not until she understood the stakes.

She returned to the journal. A final entry caught her eye, written in hurried, almost panicked script:

"If they find you with this, it will mark you. Hide the book. Hide yourself. Follow the rules, but never lose your mind. The Obedience Code contains the knowledge to survive—but also the power to destroy. Be wise, Lila. Be careful."

Her fingers trembled. "Destroy... power to destroy..." she whispered. "He wasn't exaggerating. This... this is serious."

The rain intensified, hammering against the window as if urging her to act. Lila realized she couldn't stay idle. Every moment she delayed could be dangerous. And yet, fear warred with determination—fear of the unknown, fear of the organization, fear of what she might become.

Finally, she closed the journal and placed it beside *The Obedience Code*. She stared at the black leather cover. It seemed to pulse, almost alive. She knew, instinctively, that the next step was clear: she had to decipher the rules, understand the Code, and uncover the truth about the organization her father had feared so deeply.

And somewhere, deep in the shadows beyond her window, she felt the faintest movement—like a presence waiting, observing, measuring her resolve.

Lila shivered but straightened her shoulders. "I'll do this," she whispered to herself. "I'll understand. I'll survive. And I'll find the truth."

Chapter 4: First Encounter

The sun had barely begun its descent when Lila left the library, her backpack heavier than usual with both *The Obedience Code* and her father's journal tucked carefully inside. Rain from earlier had left slick patches on the sidewalk, and the air carried the faint scent of wet asphalt and pine. She kept her eyes on the ground, trying to think, to process the new instructions she had uncovered in her father's writings.

Her thoughts were interrupted by the feeling of someone—or something—moving just behind her. She froze.

"Hello?" she called softly, glancing over her shoulder. The street was empty, save for parked cars and the occasional flickering streetlamp.

"Careful who you look for, Lila," a voice said, smooth, measured, almost too calm.

She spun around. A man stepped from the shadows near the corner store, tall and broad-shouldered, wearing a dark jacket that seemed to absorb the light around him. His face was partially hidden by the brim of a hat, but she could see sharp eyes, calculating and unblinking.

"Who... who are you?" she asked, her voice quivering despite her efforts to sound brave.

The man smiled faintly, not a friendly smile, but one that suggested he knew things he shouldn't. "Someone who notices. Someone who knows curiosity can be dangerous."

Lila's heart raced. "I—I don't understand."

"You will," he said, stepping closer, though not threateningly. "Your father left you a gift... and a warning. The Code is not meant for everyone. You have questions. That makes you a target."

Lila swallowed hard. "A target? From who?"

The man's eyes narrowed slightly. "From them. From the people who enforce obedience. You don't see them, but they see you."

She wanted to step back, but her feet felt rooted to the spot. "What... what do you want from me?"

"Nothing... yet," he said, tilting his head. "I only wanted to remind you that the path you've chosen is dangerous. Curiosity is a double-edged sword. Every step forward has consequences."

Lila's mind raced. "You... you're not one of them?"

The stranger shook his head. "I am... an observer. A guide, if you will. But be warned: there are rules. Obedience is survival. Defiance is noticed. And sometimes, resistance costs everything."

Her stomach tightened. "Why are you telling me this?"

"Because you will need it." He took a step back, his figure blending into the shadows. "Watch carefully. Trust sparingly. And remember—sometimes the right choice is the one that keeps you alive long enough to fight another day."

Before she could respond, he turned and walked into the growing darkness of the alley, disappearing as silently as he had appeared.

Lila stood frozen for a long moment, gripping her backpack straps. Questions swirled through her mind: Who was he? How did he know about the Code? And most importantly... could she trust anyone, now that she had seen the first glimpse of the organization's reach?

Shaking, she started walking home, her eyes scanning every window, every shadow. Every step felt heavier than the last. Her mind repeated the stranger's words over and over: *"Obedience is survival. Defiance is noticed. Resistance costs everything."*

By the time she reached her street, the sky had turned a bruised purple, and the first streetlights flickered on. She could feel eyes on her, though no one was there. Every shadow seemed to twitch, every passing car a possible observer.

At home, she locked the door behind her and leaned against it, taking a shaky breath. She opened her backpack and pulled out the black leather book. Its cover seemed warmer now, almost pulsing with a presence she couldn't explain.

"You're not just a book," she whispered. "You're a warning. You're... my father's legacy."

For the first time, she felt the weight of the responsibility her father had left behind. Not just to understand the Code, but to survive long enough to use it. And now, with the stranger's words echoing in her mind, she realized that understanding might not be enough. She would have to act—and carefully.

Lila traced the embossed eye on the cover with her finger. "I'll watch. I'll learn. I'll survivc," she murmured, almost as if promising herself, almost as if speaking to someone—or something—out there in the shadows.

And somewhere beyond the walls of her home, the sense of being watched didn't fade. If anything, it had only grown stronger.

Chapter 5: Unseen Eyes Watching Her

The night was still, almost unnervingly so. Lila sat at her desk, the black leather cover of *The Obedience Code* open in front of her, candles flickering along the windowsill. Every creak of the house made her jump, and her mind kept replaying the stranger's words from the previous day: *"Obedience is survival. Defiance is noticed. Resistance costs everything."*

She turned a page slowly, eyes scanning the strange symbols that had haunted her dreams. Diagrams connected circles and triangles in patterns she still didn't fully understand. She traced them with her finger, whispering, "What are you trying to teach me?"

A shadow moved across her room, subtle but distinct. Lila froze. Her pulse pounded in her ears.

"Hello?" she called, voice barely above a whisper. No answer came, only the soft scratching of rain against the window.

She swallowed hard and leaned back in her chair. *I'm imagining it. Just nerves,* she told herself.

But then, something on her desk shifted slightly. Not the book—she had placed her hands firmly on it—but a small envelope she hadn't noticed before.

Her fingers trembled as she picked it up. There was no stamp, no return address. Just her name, written in careful, angular handwriting she didn't recognize.

Opening it, she found a single sheet of paper:

"We see you. Be careful. Not everything—or everyone—is as it seems."

Lila's breath caught. She looked toward the window again, scanning the shadows outside. The street was empty. Yet a prickling sensation crawled along her neck. *Eyes. Someone's watching.*

She sat back, trying to calm herself. "It has to be connected to the book... or my father... or both," she muttered. "But why now? Why me?"

Her phone buzzed, breaking the tense silence. A notification from Mara: *You've been quiet. Everything okay?*

Lila typed carefully, *Yeah... just tired.* She couldn't risk telling anyone else—not yet.

For the next hour, she tried to focus on the book, scanning diagrams and annotations, but every shadow, every flicker of candlelight, pulled her attention away. She caught herself glancing toward the corner of her room, imagining shapes moving just beyond her vision.

Then it happened. The softest creak of the floorboards.

She froze, heart hammering. Her mind raced through every logical explanation: the old house settling, the wind shifting the floorboards, her imagination. But none of it felt right.

A whisper of movement drew her eyes to the window. Across the street, in the darkened alley beside the neighbor's garage, a figure stood still, half-hidden in shadows. Lila's stomach tightened. She ducked down, pressing the book to her chest.

The figure didn't move. It didn't make a sound. And then, as suddenly as it had appeared, it was gone.

Lila exhaled shakily, leaning against the desk. "Okay," she whispered, "you're being paranoid. But... maybe not."

She opened the book again, trying to concentrate on the symbols. Her eyes scanned a diagram showing a network of nodes, lines connecting each in intricate patterns. Tiny marginal notes read:

"Observe first. Trust sparingly. Resistance is monitored."

Her hands trembled. *Resistance is monitored...* The thought made her stomach churn. *They're everywhere... even here.*

She knew she couldn't ignore the feeling any longer. The organization her father had warned about wasn't some distant threat. It was close, active, and watching her every move.

For the first time, she realized that understanding the Code wasn't enough. She had to anticipate, to hide, to act carefully. Survival meant more than curiosity—it meant awareness, vigilance, and, sometimes, restraint.

She hugged the book tightly, whispering, "I'll watch. I'll learn. And I'll survive. But I won't be their pawn."

The rain tapped against the window again, a soft, rhythmic reminder that the night—and the shadows within it—was far from over.

And somewhere beyond the walls of her room, she knew eyes remained, unseen but unmistakably present, observing every move she made.

Chapter 6: Testing a Minor Obedience Rule

The morning sun filtered through Lila's bedroom curtains, casting golden streaks across the floor. She sat cross-legged on her bed, *The Obedience Code* open in front of her. Today, she had made a decision: she would test one of the minor obedience rules her father had annotated in the margins.

"Influence small decisions first. Observe reactions. Adjust carefully."

Her stomach twisted. *Small decisions... like what?*

Lila's mind immediately went to school. She thought of Mara, her best friend, always joking and chatting about trivial things. Could she test the rule on her? The thought made her pulse quicken. It felt risky, maybe even wrong, but curiosity overpowered caution.

At lunch, Lila sat across from Mara, carefully placing the journal and book in her backpack. Mara leaned forward, munching on a sandwich.

"So... what did you do yesterday? You were gone all morning," Mara asked casually.

Lila forced a smile. "Just... catching up on homework."

Mara raised an eyebrow. "Uh-huh. You look kind of... serious."

Lila bit her lip, thinking of the rule. *Influence small decisions.* She decided to try something simple. "Hey, Mara, do you want to swap lunches today? I have chips, you have the cookies, right?"

Mara blinked. "Uh... sure, why not?" She handed over the cookies.

Lila stared for a moment, startled. *It worked.*

Her pulse quickened. She tried another small nudge. "Also... um... can you pass me your notebook? I want to check my notes against yours for class."

Mara handed over the notebook without hesitation. "Wow, you're really on top of things today."

Lila's mind spun. *Just a minor rule... nothing major...* She tried to remind herself to stay careful. But inside, a part of her felt exhilarated—powerful in a way she hadn't expected.

Later, walking home, she replayed the lunch interactions in her mind. The rule worked. But so did the unease curling in her chest. *Was this... ethical?* She wondered. *Or am I... manipulating someone?*

Back in her room, she opened the book again, tracing the diagrams that seemed to map human behavior like a science. She read a margin note:

"Even minor influence leaves traces. Observe them."

Lila shivered. *Traces... of what? Of me? Of them?*

Her phone buzzed. A text from Mara: *Thanks for the cookies swap! You're weird today... but fun.*

Lila typed back carefully, *No problem.*

Even the casual joke felt like a confirmation that the rule had worked. She leaned back against her bed, hugging the book. The thrill of success mixed uneasily with guilt.

Influence is power... but at what cost?

She glanced toward her window, where shadows still lingered from the night before. Someone—or something—was watching, always. Lila realized that her first experiment had not gone unnoticed.

Her thoughts went to the stranger from the alley. *Did he see that? Was he... testing me?*

A soft creak in the house made her flinch. She pressed the book to her chest and whispered, "I'll be careful. I have to be. But I need to know... I need to understand the Code."

The morning stretched into afternoon as Lila scribbled notes, recording observations and reactions, documenting every minor effect her actions had produced. Each observation was a reminder: knowledge was dangerous, curiosity more so, and obedience—whether to rules or to her own moral compass—was never simple.

By the time the sun dipped behind the rooftops, Lila had a new resolve. She had touched the power of the Code and felt both exhilaration and fear. And now she understood something crucial: the rules weren't just instructions—they were tests, and she had passed the first one, carefully, cautiously.

But deep down, she knew the real tests were still to come.

Chapter 7: First Confrontation with Authority

The hallways of Westbrook High buzzed with the usual morning chaos—lockers slamming, chatter bouncing off the walls, the faint squeak of sneakers on polished floors. Lila tried to keep her head down, backpack snug on her shoulders, *The Obedience Code* tucked safely inside. Her mind, however, was anything but quiet.

She replayed yesterday's lunch experiment over and over. The thrill of minor influence still lingered, but so did the nagging worry: *Did someone notice?*

Her first-period class, English, started like any other. Mr. Hensley, a tall man with a neatly trimmed beard and sharp eyes, paced the front of the room. He stopped mid-step and stared directly at her.

"Miss Carter," he said, his voice smooth but with an edge that made her stomach tighten, "I need to speak with you after class."

Her pulse quickened. *After class... what did I do?* She nodded, trying to appear calm.

The lesson dragged, each tick of the clock a reminder that she would soon face whatever this was. When the final bell rang, she packed her things slowly, waiting for the rest of the students to leave.

Mr. Hensley waited by the door. "Lila, close the door," he instructed.

She obeyed, heart thudding. "Yes, sir."

He leaned against his desk, arms crossed. "I've noticed some... unusual behavior from you lately."

Lila's mind raced. *Unusual behavior? The lunch swap?* She kept her face neutral. "I don't... understand, sir."

He gave her a piercing look. "You have a way of influencing those around you, Miss Carter. Friends, peers... even teachers notice subtle shifts in behavior. You may not realize it, but these actions have consequences."

Lila's throat tightened. "I… I didn't mean to—"

"Intent doesn't matter," he interrupted. "Rules exist for a reason. Compliance ensures order. Deviations… are observed."

A flicker of recognition shot through her. *Compliance… observed… just like the book.* Her pulse raced. Had he noticed her little experiment? Or was this something larger?

"I understand, sir," she said carefully, forcing herself to sound calm. *Observe first. Obey selectively.*

He nodded slowly, though his gaze didn't soften. "See that you do. The smallest choice can ripple outward. I suggest caution."

As Lila walked out of the classroom, her backpack felt heavier than ever. She pressed her hand over the black leather book inside. The Code was real, and she was only beginning to see its reach.

Outside the classroom, Mara caught up to her, cheerful as ever. "You okay? You looked like Mr. Hensley just yelled at you or something."

Lila forced a smile. "Yeah… just a talk about… class participation."

Mara frowned slightly, unconvinced, but didn't press. Lila realized how fragile trust had become. Even a minor deviation, an experiment in influence, had drawn attention.

Later, walking home, Lila replayed the conversation in her mind. *Every action leaves traces. Observed. Monitored.* The book's warnings echoed louder than ever.

By the time she reached her room, the shadows outside had deepened. She opened *The Obedience Code*, flipping through diagrams and marginal notes:

"Every choice is visible. Resistance is detected. Obedience ensures survival."

Her fingers trembled. The lesson was clear: survival wasn't just about understanding the rules. It was about learning when to obey, when to resist, and how to navigate the unseen eyes that monitored every step.

Sitting at her desk, Lila whispered to herself, "I'll follow carefully… but I won't lose myself. Not yet."

Outside, the quiet hum of the street was broken by the faintest rustle of movement, just beyond the glow of the streetlamp. Unseen, always watching, the eyes of the organization lingered.

And now, more than ever, Lila knew she had entered a world where even small choices could have dangerous consequences.

Chapter 8: Discovering That Friends May Be Informants

The next morning, Lila met Mara at their usual spot in the school courtyard. The sky was a pale gray, the air crisp and biting, and a thin breeze carried the chatter of students walking to class. Lila forced herself to appear casual, but her mind was already turning over the stranger's warnings and Mr. Hensley's words.

"Morning! You look... tired," Mara said, nudging her playfully. "Late night studying?"

"Something like that," Lila replied, keeping her voice neutral. Her eyes scanned the courtyard, unconsciously noting shadows and people lingering where they shouldn't.

As they walked to class, Lila noticed Mara pausing repeatedly, glancing behind them. "You okay?" she asked.

Mara laughed nervously. "Yeah, just... uh, thinking about homework. Weird dreams last night."

Lila frowned. Something about the way Mara said it—hesitant, almost too careful—set off alarms in her mind. She tried to shake it off. *Maybe I'm overthinking.*

But then, during first-period English, she overheard a snippet of conversation from Mara to another student near the back of the classroom.

"...Yeah, I saw her with the book. Weird, right?"

Lila froze. *The book... she's talking about the Code.*

Her stomach churned. The words weren't meant for her ears, but now they were. Her best friend, the one person she thought she could trust, might have been reporting her actions—or worse, unwittingly passing information to someone else.

She forced herself to breathe slowly, keeping her face calm. She didn't react immediately, but the seed of suspicion had been planted.

After class, Lila pulled Mara aside in the empty hallway. "Hey... can I ask you something?"

Mara looked at her, eyes wide. "Sure, what's up?"

Lila's voice was careful, measured. "Have you... told anyone about the book? About what I've been doing?"

Mara blinked. "What? No! Of course not! Why would I—"

"Are you sure?" Lila pressed, trying to read her expressions, noticing the micro-facial cues her father had taught her to watch in his journals—tiny twitches, a slight hesitation, an almost imperceptible narrowing of the eyes.

Mara hesitated longer than expected. "I... I didn't mean anything by it. Just... some kids were talking, and I thought—"

Lila's heart sank. It wasn't outright betrayal, but it was enough to plant doubt. The organization's influence could be subtle, even indirect. Mara might not even realize she was passing information.

"I need you to be careful," Lila said softly, her voice steady despite the tension. "Some people notice... and some people report. Even without knowing it."

Mara's lips pressed together. "Okay... I'll be careful."

Lila nodded, forcing herself to smile. On the surface, everything looked normal. But underneath, the world had shifted. Friends could be informants. Trust could be weaponized. And now, more than ever, she had to rely on her wits—and the Code—to survive.

Later that evening, Lila opened the book again, scanning the annotations and diagrams. Her father had warned her about trust, observation, and the danger of subtle betrayal. She realized that the first real test wasn't about obedience rules—it was about knowing whom to trust, and learning that sometimes even friends could unknowingly become threats.

She closed the book, hugging it tightly. "I have to be smarter," she whispered. "Faster. I can't let anyone—or anything—use me."

From outside her window, a shadow shifted. Someone was still watching. Someone always was.

And Lila knew that learning to navigate friendships, alliances, and betrayals would be just as important as mastering the rules of the Code itself.

Chapter 9: First Coded Message from Father

The evening was unusually quiet. Lila sat at her desk, *The Obedience Code* and her father's journal open side by side. The earlier tension with Mara weighed on her mind, but there was something more pressing gnawing at her—a feeling that the organization, or someone connected to it, was watching her every move.

She rifled through the journal, scanning for patterns, notes, anything that might guide her next steps. That's when she noticed a small envelope tucked between two pages she had read dozens of times before. It wasn't new, but she hadn't seen it. The envelope was thin, made of worn paper, with her father's unmistakable handwriting scrawled across it:

"For Lila—when the time is right."

Her hands trembled as she tore it open. Inside was a single sheet of paper covered in symbols, numbers, and letters arranged in a way that didn't make sense at first glance.

"Coded message," she whispered.

She spread the paper across her desk, comparing the symbols with those in *The Obedience Code*. Slowly, a pattern began to emerge. The spirals and arrows in the margins corresponded to letters, forming words when traced carefully.

"Trust only what can be verified. Step lightly. Observe who observes you."

Her pulse quickened. She recognized the subtle echo of the stranger's warning and Mr. Hensley's words: observation, surveillance, obedience.

There was more. Another line of symbols mapped to coordinates—a location in town she vaguely recognized from a map her father had kept: an abandoned library on the edge of the old district.

Lila whispered, almost afraid she would say it aloud: "He wants me to go... there?"

Her mind raced. *Why now? Why this location? Is it safe... or a trap?* The questions tangled in her head, but the coded message didn't leave room for hesitation. Her father had always emphasized the importance of taking action, even when the risk was high.

She glanced out her window at the darkened street. Shadows clung to the edges of the buildings, and every movement made her flinch. The message pulsed in her mind: observe who observes you. Step lightly. Trust sparingly.

Her phone buzzed, breaking the tense silence. A text from Mara: *You okay? You seem... distracted.*

Lila stared at the screen, debating whether to respond. She typed carefully, *I'm fine,* and deleted it, unsure if even casual messages could be monitored.

Returning her focus to the coded message, she noticed a small note at the bottom:

"If discovered, destroy evidence. Obedience is survival—but knowledge is power. Decide which matters most."

Lila's hands shook as she folded the paper and tucked it safely into her journal. She realized that her father had left her more than instructions—he had left her a test.

A test of intelligence. Of courage. Of moral conviction.

She whispered to herself, voice steady despite the fear: "I'll go. I'll see. I'll understand. And I'll survive."

Outside, the streetlights flickered. A shadow moved past her window, deliberate and unhurried. Someone—or something—was still watching. But this time, Lila felt a strange sense of determination. She wasn't just being observed; she was learning to anticipate.

And the first coded message was just the beginning.

Chapter 10: Researching the Organization Online

The glow of her laptop filled Lila's bedroom, casting shadows across the walls as rain tapped softly against the window. She sat cross-legged on her bed, *The Obedience Code* and her father's journal beside her, the coded message folded neatly inside the journal.

Her fingers hovered over the keyboard, heart pounding. She had a location, a warning, and cryptic instructions—but no context for the organization her father had warned about.

Time to see what the internet knows, she thought.

Her first searches were vague: "Obedience societies," "hidden control networks," "influence experiments." Most results were conspiracy theories or unrelated forums, but patterns began to emerge. Mentions of secret councils, clandestine training programs, and anecdotal reports of manipulation filtered through ordinary lives.

"Okay... that's... unsettling," Lila muttered, scrolling through a forum post detailing unusual behavioral experiments in small towns across the country.

Her pulse quickened when she saw a familiar symbol—an eye embedded in interlocking triangles—the same glyph repeated in her father's book. It had a name: *The Custodians.*

Her fingers shook as she typed, "The Custodians influence obedience in schools and communities." The search results were scarce, fragmented, and heavily redacted, almost as if someone had tried to erase their traces.

Then a chat window popped up from an anonymous user:

I see you're looking for answers. Be careful. Trust no one.

Lila froze, staring at the screen. Her first instinct was to close it, but curiosity and the urgency her father had instilled made her pause. "Who... are you?" she typed cautiously.

The reply came almost instantly:

I know what you seek. The book is not just a record. It's a guide. The organization watches. Observe them. Learn before they learn you.

Her stomach churned. This was exactly what her father had warned: unseen eyes, covert influence, and the ever-present danger of exposure.

"Okay… I get it," she typed. "But I need more. What is The Custodians?"

The response was short:

Patience. First, survive. Then learn the rules. Not everyone who watches is an enemy, but everyone has a cost. The Code is your shield and your weapon.

Lila leaned back, gripping her laptop. Her mind whirled with questions: Who had sent this? Could she trust them? And most importantly, how far-reaching was this organization her father had feared?

The rain outside intensified, drumming against the windowpane. Shadows stretched across her room, and for the first time, she felt a pang of fear mingled with exhilaration. The world she had glimpsed in the book was bigger, more dangerous, and more real than she had imagined.

She whispered to herself, almost as a promise, "I'll find them. I'll learn the rules. And I'll survive. No matter what."

With renewed determination, she began compiling notes, screenshots, and patterns. Every symbol, every fragment of information, became a thread she could pull. She realized that understanding the organization required more than observation—it required intelligence, patience, and courage.

And somewhere, deep in the shadows of her digital search, the organization noticed her.

But Lila didn't care. Not yet.

The first step in unraveling the Code was research, and she was ready to dive deeper, no matter the risk.

Chapter 11: Manipulative Experiment in Town

The afternoon sun cast long shadows across the streets of Lila's neighborhood. She walked carefully, backpack snug on her shoulders, *The Obedience Code* tucked safely inside. Her eyes scanned every passerby, every parked car. The rain had stopped, but the air still carried a damp, earthy smell that made her senses feel sharper than usual.

She had chosen today for her small reconnaissance: observing patterns in the town to detect any signs of the organization's influence. Her father's journal and the coded message had prepared her for subtlety—sometimes, the tests weren't blatant, but manipulations so fine that only a careful observer could notice.

At the corner of Main and 5th, she spotted it: a small group of people standing near the fountain, acting oddly. Their movements were synchronized in small ways—shuffling feet at the same time, glancing at one another before speaking, slight nods exchanged like a silent protocol.

This... is no ordinary gathering, Lila whispered to herself.

She crouched behind a lamppost, pulling out her phone to record discreetly. One man approached the fountain, holding a clipboard. He spoke softly to the group, giving instructions they followed without question.

They're practicing obedience... on ordinary citizens, she realized, stomach twisting.

Her attention shifted to a teenager trying to resist—moving against the flow, hesitating to follow an instruction. Immediately, two others subtly nudged him back into alignment. Lila's pulse raced. The experiment was real, precise, and unrelenting.

She typed a quick note into her journal: *Manipulation confirmed. Observed group responding to cues. Resistance punished subtly. Rules applied in public spaces.*

Suddenly, a shadow fell across her shoulder. She spun around. A man in a dark jacket stood there, face partially obscured by a hood. His gaze was piercing, evaluating.

"You're watching," he said, his voice low but commanding.

Lila's heart thumped. She tried to appear calm. "I'm just... observing," she replied carefully.

He tilted his head, studying her. "Curiosity is dangerous. But it's also... useful. Keep notes. Record what you see. But step lightly, or they will notice."

Before she could respond, he stepped back into the crowd, disappearing as silently as he had appeared.

Lila crouched for a moment, trying to steady her breathing. The encounter had confirmed her worst fears: the organization's influence wasn't limited to symbols or rules in a book—it was active in her town, manipulating behavior in real time, testing obedience and resistance in unsuspecting citizens.

As she walked home, her mind whirled with possibilities. *They're everywhere... even here. And I'm part of their test now.*

Back in her room, she opened the book and traced the symbols on the page, whispering, "Every action has a reaction. Every rule observed. They're testing me... like they tested everyone else."

She hugged the book tightly, the weight of her father's legacy pressing down on her. The Code wasn't just about survival—it was about understanding, outsmarting, and navigating a world where obedience was enforced, loyalty was tested, and defiance came at a price.

And Lila knew that she could no longer watch from the shadows. To survive, to protect herself and those she cared about, she would have to step into the game—carefully, strategically, and fully aware of the eyes always upon her.

Chapter 12: The Mysterious Letter Warning Her Not to Read Further

That evening, Lila sat at her desk, reviewing the notes she had taken while observing the obedience experiment in town. The room was quiet, except for the soft hum of her laptop and the occasional rustle of pages from her father's journal. She had barely touched her dinner, too consumed with the implications of what she had witnessed.

A soft knock at the window startled her. Lila froze, then cautiously approached, peering through the blinds. Nothing. Just the shadows of the evening settling over the street.

Shaking her head, she returned to her desk, only to find an envelope lying across the black leather cover of *The Obedience Code*. It hadn't been there when she left the room.

Her heart raced as she picked it up. The envelope was plain, with no stamp, no return address—just her name, written in a careful, almost menacing script.

Hands trembling, she opened it. Inside was a single piece of thick paper, with a short, direct message typed in bold letters:

"Stop. Do not read further. Obedience is survival. Curiosity can kill. The Code is not meant for you—yet. Heed this warning, or you will be next."

Lila's pulse thundered in her chest. Her mind raced. *Next? What does that mean? Are they threatening me?*

She grabbed the book instinctively, pressing it to her chest. "I... I can't stop now," she whispered. "I have to understand... I have to know."

A sudden creak behind her made her spin around. The shadows in her room seemed deeper, almost alive. "Who's there?" she demanded, voice shaky but defiant.

Silence. Only the soft tap of rain against the window answered.

She sat back down, staring at the letter. Every instinct screamed to obey, to put the book away, to lock the room and pretend she had never seen it. But another voice, stronger and sharper, echoed in her mind—her father's voice, from his journal:

"Curiosity is the first step toward survival. Fear is the first test. Choose wisely, but do not let fear dictate your path."

Lila took a deep breath. Her hands were still shaking, but her resolve hardened. "I'll be careful," she whispered to herself. "But I won't stop. I can't stop. I need to learn the Code... to survive."

She tucked the letter away into the journal, making a note of it in the margins: *Warning received. Risk acknowledged. Proceeding.*

Outside, the streetlights flickered. Shadows lingered longer than they should, and she couldn't shake the feeling of eyes on her. But Lila knew one thing for certain: the warning was meant to intimidate, to deter her.

And she wouldn't be deterred.

The Obedience Code wasn't just a book. It was a path—treacherous, dangerous, but necessary. And Lila was determined to walk it, no matter the cost.

Chapter 13: Deciding to Ignore the Warning

The morning sun filtered through her curtains, casting long, sharp lines across Lila's bedroom floor. Her father's book lay open on her desk, the mysterious letter from the previous night tucked carefully beside it. For hours, she had stared at the warning, rereading the words over and over:

"Stop. Do not read further. Obedience is survival... you will be next."

Her pulse still raced at the memory, but the warning did not scare her as much as it intrigued her. It was a challenge, a test. And Lila had never been good at ignoring challenges.

She touched the black leather cover of the book. "I can't stop now," she whispered. "I need to know... I have to understand."

Her phone buzzed—a text from Mara: *Are you okay? You seem... off.*

Lila hesitated before typing: *I'm fine. Just busy.* She didn't dare explain. She wasn't ready for anyone else to know how dangerous her path had become.

Sitting at her desk, she opened *The Obedience Code*, flipping to the section her father had last marked. Strange symbols danced across the page, diagrams of human behavior intertwined with annotations in her father's precise handwriting.

A phrase caught her eye:

"True power is in knowledge. Obedience teaches survival, but understanding teaches control. Fear those who demand obedience without question."

She closed her eyes, letting the words sink in. The warning wasn't just about reading the book—it was about *choosing to act despite danger.* And Lila had made her choice.

I will not be their pawn, she thought. *I will learn. I will survive.*

Her hands shook slightly as she began transcribing notes, decoding the symbols, and comparing them with the lessons she had observed in town. Every scribble on the page, every mark her father had left, became a stepping stone toward understanding the rules of the organization—and how to navigate them safely.

The shadows outside her window shifted, reminding her that she was not alone. Someone—or something—was always watching. But for the first time, Lila felt a measure of control. She wasn't hiding; she was learning.

By nightfall, she had a strategy forming. She would follow the Code carefully, testing each rule, observing every reaction. She would obey when survival required it, resist when it mattered most, and never lose sight of the bigger picture.

The warning letter lay folded on her desk, a reminder of the danger she faced. She picked it up, held it to her chest, then placed it carefully in her drawer.

Fear is a tool. Fear is a test. And I will pass.

Outside, the street remained quiet, but the sense of being observed lingered like a cold whisper. Lila knew this was only the beginning. By choosing to ignore the warning, she had stepped fully into the path her father had left her—a path filled with danger, secrets, and the constant challenge of survival.

And she would not turn back.

Chapter 14: First Moral Dilemma – Obey or Resist Minor Law

The next day, Lila walked into Westbrook High feeling the weight of the book tucked into her backpack. Her father's coded lessons were still fresh in her mind, and the warning letter lingered like a shadow she couldn't shake. Every glance from teachers, every passing student seemed to carry hidden scrutiny.

During history class, Mr. Hensley handed out a surprise assignment. "Everyone will remain seated until the instructions are fully read," he said, scanning the room with his usual sharp gaze. "No exceptions."

Lila's pulse quickened. She knew that following the rule was safe, but her curiosity whispered otherwise. Her father's journal had often emphasized testing limits in subtle ways, observing the outcomes without drawing immediate attention.

As Mr. Hensley explained the exercise, she noticed that her friend, Jonah, was quietly passing notes under the table. He scribbled a question to another student, subtly violating the rule.

Her mind raced. *If I report him, I obey the authority. If I don't... I resist. But what about fairness? What about morality?*

Lila hesitated. Then, a thought struck her: *The Code isn't just about obedience—it's about consequences and observation.*

She made a choice. Instead of reporting Jonah, she subtly slid a note back to him: *Careful. Eyes everywhere.* It wasn't disobedience, but it was a warning, a quiet act of subtle resistance.

Mr. Hensley's eyes swept the classroom, but he didn't notice. Lila exhaled slowly, heart racing. She had resisted without direct confrontation, following the principle of calculated action.

After class, Jonah whispered, "Thanks... I don't know how you knew."

Lila smiled faintly, keeping her voice low. "Just pay attention."

Alone later, she wrote in her journal: *Lesson 1: Obey when necessary. Resist when meaningful. Every action has consequences. Observers are always present.*

She realized for the first time that obeying blindly was survival—but understanding when to resist, when to act, and when to conceal was power. And the line between right and wrong was not always clear.

Outside, shadows lingered, and the sense of unseen eyes persisted. Lila knew the organization was watching, but she also understood something crucial: mastering the Code meant balancing morality with strategy, learning which rules could be bent, and which could not.

Tonight, she would dream again of symbols and diagrams, of patterns hidden in plain sight. And tomorrow, she would face another test—another moral and practical challenge in the intricate web her father had revealed.

She pressed the book to her chest and whispered: "I will learn. I will observe. I will survive. And I will never be just another pawn."

Chapter 15: First Clues of the Organization's Control Over Family Members

The morning air smelled of damp leaves as Lila walked toward the old family home. Her father's death still weighed heavily on her, and the black leather book in her backpack felt heavier than ever. Something in the coded message had suggested that the organization's influence extended beyond the public sphere, into personal lives—and now she was beginning to see why.

In the kitchen, her mother hummed quietly, preparing breakfast. Lila noticed how methodically she arranged the utensils, placing them with a precision that seemed unnatural, almost ritualistic. A chill ran down her spine.

"Mom... have you ever noticed how Dad... organized everything before he left?" Lila asked, trying to sound casual.

Her mother froze for a moment, then forced a small smile. "He was thorough, always careful. Why do you ask?"

Lila hesitated, her mind racing. Her father's notes had hinted at subtle pressures applied to family members—ways the organization ensured obedience without open confrontation. Could her mother have been influenced, even unconsciously?

Later, while sorting through her father's old desk, Lila found another envelope, hidden beneath a drawer. Inside was a photograph of her mother standing at a town meeting several years ago, surrounded by people wearing symbols she had seen in *The Obedience Code*. A note on the back read:

"Observe the familiar. Trust cautiously. Influence begins at home."

Her pulse quickened. The organization wasn't just shaping strangers—it had started with her own family. Every subtle action, every habit, could have been guided or monitored.

Her mind raced with questions. Had her mother's decisions been her own? Had her father resisted silently, shielding them as best he could? And how many choices in her life had already been influenced without her knowing?

Determined to understand, Lila began cataloging small, unusual patterns she noticed: behaviors that seemed slightly off, repetitive habits, or reactions that didn't match the situation. Each observation was a clue, a potential window into the subtle reach of the organization.

That night, lying in bed, Lila whispered to herself: "The Code doesn't just teach survival... it teaches awareness. And if it can touch my family, it can touch anyone. I have to be ready."

The shadows outside seemed deeper than usual, pressing against the windows, reminding her that even the people closest to her might be pawns—or under observation. Lila hugged the book to her chest.

She had learned something vital: the fight wasn't just out there in the world—it began at home, in the small choices and unseen pressures shaping the lives of those she loved.

And if she wanted to survive and uncover the truth, she would have to understand the Code better than anyone else—and prepare for the tests yet to come.

Chapter 16: Lila's First Dream Revealing Hidden Truths

The night was silent, except for the faint hum of the streetlights outside her window. Lila tossed restlessly in bed, the weight of the day pressing on her chest. Her mind, full of observations and unanswered questions, refused to settle.

Finally, sleep claimed her—but it brought no rest.

She found herself in a strange landscape, a city both familiar and foreign. Buildings twisted at impossible angles, streets looping back on themselves. Shadows moved independently, slipping along walls and corners as if alive. And everywhere she looked, symbols from *The Obedience Code* floated in the air: eyes, triangles, spirals.

A voice echoed around her, distorted but unmistakably her father's:

"Observe what is hidden, Lila. Obedience is not just action—it is perception. Trust only what can be verified."

She turned to follow the voice, moving through the city streets. Figures appeared in the shadows, familiar faces distorted: her mother, Mara, even Mr. Hensley. Each held a clipboard, nodding to one another as if coordinating. Lila's stomach twisted.

"They are everywhere," the voice continued. *"Even those you love may be influenced. Detect patterns. Anticipate reactions. Choose carefully."*

Ahead, she saw a door covered in interlocking symbols. She reached for the handle, and the door swung open to reveal a room filled with clocks—all ticking at different speeds, some forwards, some backwards. At the center, a figure resembling her father sat, writing notes in a book identical to *The Obedience Code*.

"Lila," he said softly, "the Code is not just a guide. It is a map of behavior, of influence, of choice. Understanding it means seeing the unseen, hearing the unspoken. And surviving it means knowing when to obey... and when to resist."

She reached out, but the figure vanished, leaving only the ticking of the clocks. Time warped around her, and she felt an urgent pull: every decision, every minor action, had consequences she couldn't yet calculate.

Suddenly, she woke with a gasp, the book clutched tightly to her chest. Her heart pounded, her body drenched in sweat. The room was dark, shadows stretching across the walls, eerily similar to the dream city.

Lila exhaled slowly, trying to steady her racing mind. The dream was more than a nightmare—it was a lesson, a warning, and a guide all at once. The Code was alive in a sense she hadn't understood before: it was a living framework of human behavior, observation, and influence.

She opened her father's journal and wrote: *Lesson from dream: Obedience is visible. Resistance is measured. Trust cautiously. Observe all.*

Outside, shadows shifted as if in response to her newfound resolve. Lila realized that dreams could reveal truths she couldn't see while awake, and that the organization's influence was not limited to daylight.

She pressed the book to her chest, whispering: "I see now. The path is dangerous... but I will follow it. I will learn the rules, and I will survive."

Chapter 17: Shadow Following Her Home

The evening air was heavy with the scent of rain and damp earth as Lila walked home from school. Her backpack felt unusually heavy, not from books, but from the weight of knowledge she carried—the book, her father's notes, and the secrets she had uncovered about the organization.

She glanced over her shoulder. At first, she saw nothing. But after a few steps, a subtle movement caught her eye—a figure, lingering near the corner of the street. Dressed in dark clothing, the stranger's face was obscured by a hood, but Lila's instincts screamed that they were watching.

Not a dream this time, she thought, heart thudding.

She adjusted her pace, taking a detour down side streets, looping through alleys she knew well. Each time she glanced back, the shadow was still there, matching her movements with unnerving precision.

Her pulse quickened. "Who are you? What do you want?" she whispered under her breath, careful not to speak too loudly.

The figure didn't respond. They simply mirrored her path, always just far enough behind to remain unseen by others, yet close enough to be undeniable.

Lila ducked into a small park, hoping to lose them among the benches and trees. She crouched behind a bush, chest heaving. The figure slowed, stopping just outside the light cast by a streetlamp.

Lila's fingers instinctively touched the book in her backpack. *Obedience is survival... but knowledge is power.* Her father's words echoed in her mind.

The figure remained motionless for a few tense moments, then disappeared down a side street as silently as they had appeared.

Lila exhaled, trembling. The encounter confirmed something she had long suspected: the organization's reach was closer, more immediate, and more personal than she had imagined. They were watching her, testing her, perhaps even guiding her through fear.

Back in her room, she locked the door, sliding the book onto her desk. Shadows still danced along the walls, cast by the flickering streetlights outside. Lila realized survival meant constant vigilance, not just understanding the Code but anticipating those who enforced it.

She whispered to herself: "I see you... and I won't be controlled. Not now. Not ever."

Her reflection in the window caught her eye, and for the first time, she felt a shiver of both fear and determination. She wasn't just being observed—she was being tested. And Lila knew that the first step to surviving was recognizing the shadow, learning its pattern, and planning her next move carefully.

Chapter 18: Experimenting with Obedience Rules in Secret

The house was quiet, the soft tick of the clock echoing through the room. Lila sat cross-legged on the floor, the black leather cover of *The Obedience Code* open before her. Her father's notes sprawled across the desk, filled with diagrams, symbols, and instructions she had spent weeks deciphering.

She picked up a small notebook, a place to document her experiments. Tonight, she decided, would be the first time she tested the principles in a controlled environment—carefully, strategically, with minimal risk.

Her first target: simple obedience in everyday interactions. She set up a small experiment with her younger neighbor, Tommy, who often ignored instructions while playing in the yard.

"Tommy," she said softly, kneeling near the fence, "can you bring me that ball?"

He hesitated, glancing toward his mother. Lila ignored the outside observers and spoke again, calmly but firmly, "Now, please."

To her surprise, he obeyed immediately, handing over the ball without protest. She noted the response: *Tone matters. Authority is subtle but effective when confidence is projected.*

Next, she experimented on herself. Following the Code, she set small rules: keep the lights off for one hour, avoid using her phone, follow a strict pattern of actions around the house. Each act of self-imposed obedience sharpened her awareness. She felt a strange sense of control, a calm focus she had never experienced before.

Lila paused, reflecting. "Obedience isn't just survival," she whispered to herself. "It's learning patterns. Testing limits. Observing reactions. Understanding behavior gives power."

Her experiment took a bolder step. She wrote a small instruction and slipped it under her mother's door: *Place the red cup on the table by 7:00*

PM. She waited, heart pounding. Her mother complied without question, leaving the cup exactly as instructed. Lila jotted it down carefully: *Subtle influence works even on familiar subjects.*

By the end of the night, her notebook was full of observations, small victories, and careful notes on human response. She realized that the Code wasn't abstract—it was practical, measurable, and applicable in real life.

Sitting back, she whispered to herself, pressing the book to her chest, "If I can master these rules, even in small ways, I can anticipate... I can survive. And one day, I can fight back."

Outside, shadows lingered beyond her window, but Lila no longer flinched. Tonight, she had begun to wield the principles of the Code with intention, testing obedience, control, and influence—steps toward understanding a system far bigger than she had imagined.

Chapter 19: Learning That Her Closest Friend Might Be Under the Organization's Influence

The next morning, Lila met Mara at their usual spot in the school courtyard. The air was crisp, carrying the scent of fallen leaves, but Lila barely noticed. Her mind was racing, recalling subtle behaviors she had observed over the past weeks.

"Hey, Lila! You look... tired," Mara said, smiling but with a hint of unease in her eyes.

"Morning," Lila replied cautiously, keeping her voice neutral. Her father's notes on observation and reading micro-expressions played through her mind. Something was off.

As they walked to class, Lila noticed Mara glancing repeatedly over her shoulder, fidgeting with the strap of her backpack. It was subtle, but familiar—too familiar, reminiscent of the patterns she had seen in the obedience experiments around town.

Could she be influenced? Or worse... reporting me? Lila's stomach twisted.

Later, during lunch, Lila watched Mara closely. The girl laughed at jokes she hadn't heard, nodded at conversations she wasn't part of, and occasionally scribbled on a notepad, quickly hiding it when Lila looked in her direction.

Lila's pulse quickened. She decided to test her suspicion without revealing her knowledge. Pulling out a small slip of paper, she wrote a subtle instruction: *Leave your backpack on the bench and go to the library alone.*

She placed it where Mara would see it and observed from a distance. Mara paused, glanced around nervously, then obeyed immediately, walking toward the library without a word.

Lila's heart sank. Her closest friend—someone she had trusted implicitly—might already be under influence or being monitored. The realization was sharp, cutting deeper than any fear she had felt so far.

After school, Lila confronted Mara privately in a quiet hallway. "Mara... have you been... following instructions? Have you been... told what to do?" Her voice was low but steady, masking the rising panic.

Mara hesitated, eyes darting. "I... I don't know what you mean," she replied, forcing a smile that didn't reach her eyes.

Lila studied her carefully, recalling her father's lessons: microexpressions, subtle cues, hesitation. Something was wrong. "If someone's controlling you... you have to tell me. I need to know."

Mara's shoulders tensed. She opened her mouth, then closed it, nodding slightly. "I... I can't. Not yet. I'm... scared."

The words hit Lila like a physical blow. Fear could be weaponized. Loyalty could be coerced. And sometimes, even friends could be unwilling agents of the organization.

That night, Lila wrote in her journal: *Lesson: Trust cautiously. Observation is survival. Even friends can be pawns. Prepare for deception and manipulation.*

The shadows outside her window stretched longer than usual, reminding her that no one—not even those closest—was entirely free from influence. Lila pressed the book to her chest, determination hardening within her.

I will protect myself. I will learn the rules. I will survive. And I will find a way to protect those I care about, even if they don't realize they need it.

Chapter 20: Act 1 Climax – Discovering an Underground Cell

The night air was sharp against Lila's skin as she approached the abandoned library at the edge of town. The coordinates from her father's coded message burned in her mind. Every step felt heavy, weighted with anticipation. This was no ordinary location—it was a place deliberately hidden, a threshold into the organization's inner workings.

She slipped through a side door, its rusted hinges groaning under the pressure. Inside, the air was stale and cold. Dust coated the floor, broken furniture littered the corners, and shadows clung to the walls like living creatures.

Her heart raced. *If this is what I think it is... I'm stepping directly into their world.*

Lila moved quietly, following a series of subtle markers her father had annotated in the book: arrows etched into the floor, spirals on walls, small symbols she recognized from his diagrams. Each one guided her deeper into the building.

Finally, she reached a heavy metal door, its surface etched with interlocking symbols—the same she had seen repeatedly in her father's notes. With trembling hands, she pushed it open.

Inside was a vast underground chamber, dimly lit by a row of flickering lamps. Dozens of people moved with purpose, some writing on tablets, others monitoring screens filled with data. The air was alive with quiet whispers and the hum of machinery.

Lila's eyes widened. This was a cell of the organization—real, operational, and active. The subtle power she had glimpsed in the town experiments was only the surface; here was the mechanism, the heart of the network.

Suddenly, footsteps echoed behind her. She spun around, clutching her book, but a figure stepped out of the shadows—not threatening, but calculating.

"You've come far," the stranger said, voice low and measured. "Few ever find this place. Fewer still leave with their freedom intact."

Lila's pulse thundered, but she squared her shoulders. "I need to know what this is... why it exists. And I need to understand the Code."

The figure studied her, then nodded slowly. "Then watch closely. Learn quickly. Because the organization doesn't tolerate mistakes. And neither should you."

As Lila observed the cell, the patterns she had studied—the obedience rules, the manipulations, the subtle tests—came alive. Every gesture, every interaction, every decision was part of a larger system of control. And for the first time, she understood the scale of the challenge before her.

She pressed the book to her chest. The path ahead was perilous, but clarity had arrived. Act 1 had revealed the rules, the threats, and the hidden structures. And now, with the underground cell exposed, the real battle to master the Code—and survive—was about to begin.

Chapter 21: Lila Decides to Infiltrate the Organization

The underground cell's shadows still lingered in Lila's mind as she walked home from the abandoned library. Every detail from the night—the flickering lamps, the whispers, the people moving with purpose—played in her head on a loop. She pressed the book tightly to her chest.

I can't just observe anymore, she thought. *I need to go deeper. I need to infiltrate them.*

At home, she spread *The Obedience Code* across her desk, flipping through her father's annotations. Every diagram, every note, every symbol now felt like a roadmap—not just for survival, but for penetration. She studied the hierarchy she had glimpsed: enforcers, council members, data analysts, and the unseen leaders at the top.

Her first step was to recruit an ally. She knew she couldn't do this alone. Her eyes landed on a photograph of Mara from last week—the hesitant glances, the subtle obedience patterns. Lila's pulse quickened. Could she trust her? Or had Mara already been compromised?

The next day at school, Lila cornered Jonah in the quiet corner of the library. "I need your help," she whispered. "There's... something bigger than us. I can't do this alone."

Jonah hesitated. "What are you talking about?"

"The organization," Lila said, eyes sharp. "They control everything. I've seen their cell, and I'm going to go inside. I need someone I can trust."

Jonah swallowed hard. "Are you crazy? If they catch us..."

"Exactly," Lila interrupted. "That's why I need someone smart, careful, observant. I need you. But it's optional. You can walk away now."

Jonah studied her for a long moment, then nodded. "Okay... I'm in. But you better know what you're doing."

Lila felt a flicker of hope. With a reluctant but willing ally, she began planning her first steps. She spent the night training in secret, using the Code's principles to prepare herself mentally, emotionally, and physically. Each exercise, from subtle observation to obedience testing, sharpened her senses.

By dawn, she had drafted a preliminary infiltration plan: observe without revealing, test minor rules to gauge reactions, and build credibility with the lowest-ranking members first. The risks were monumental, but Lila's resolve had never been stronger.

She whispered to herself, flipping through the book one last time: "I will learn their rules… I will bend them… and I will survive. One step at a time."

Outside, shadows still lurked at the edges of her home, silent watchers in the dark. But this time, Lila didn't flinch. She was ready to step into the game, fully aware that every choice could mean the difference between survival and being erased.

Chapter 22: Recruiting a Hesitant Ally

The school library smelled of old books and polished wood, a comforting contrast to the chaos in Lila's mind. Jonah sat at a corner table, nervously flipping through his notebook, glancing at the door every few minutes. Lila approached, careful not to draw attention.

"Hey," she whispered, sliding into the seat across from him.

Jonah looked up, eyes wary. "I've been thinking... about what you said yesterday. About the organization."

Lila nodded. "It's real, Jonah. I've seen their underground cell. They're controlling people—even people you think you can trust. And they won't hesitate to eliminate threats."

Jonah's fingers twitched on the table. "So... what exactly are you asking me to do?"

"Help me infiltrate them," Lila said, keeping her voice low. "I can't do it alone. I need someone I can observe with, someone I can trust with small risks first before escalating."

Jonah swallowed hard. "And if we get caught?"

Lila's gaze hardened. "Then we face the consequences. But if we succeed, we can learn their rules, their hierarchy, their weaknesses. And we survive."

Jonah hesitated, then nodded slowly. "Okay... but I need to know everything before I make a real commitment. No secrets."

"I'll show you what I can," Lila said, pulling *The Obedience Code* from her backpack. She flipped it open, revealing diagrams, symbols, and notes her father had left. "This is the path. It's dangerous, but methodical. We test obedience rules, observe patterns, and gather intelligence slowly. Step by step."

Jonah leaned in, eyes scanning the pages. "It's... a lot. But I get it. We could be the ones to finally understand them... to beat them at their own game."

Lila smiled faintly. "Exactly. But we have to stay cautious. Start small. Trust cautiously. Every move matters."

The bell rang, and students began filing in, oblivious to the weight of the plan being formed in the quiet corner of the library. Lila packed the book carefully, sliding it into her backpack.

"Are you sure about this?" Jonah asked quietly as they left the library.

"I've never been more certain," Lila replied. "We start small, we observe, we test. And we stay alive. That's the rule."

As they walked back to class, Lila felt a surge of resolve. Having an ally—hesitant though he might be—gave her an edge. Together, they could begin the careful work of infiltration, testing obedience rules in practice, and uncovering the organization's secrets from within.

The shadows outside the school seemed longer than usual, and Lila felt the weight of unseen eyes. But this time, she didn't flinch. She was no longer just a student; she was a strategist, ready to step into the heart of danger with an ally by her side.

Chapter 23: Training in Secrecy Using The Obedience Code

The attic above Lila's garage had been converted into a makeshift training space. Dust motes floated in the dim light, and old furniture was pushed aside to make room for maps, notebooks, and the black leather cover of *The Obedience Code*.

Jonah stood by the small table, glancing nervously at the book. "Are you sure we won't get caught? What if someone sees us?"

Lila shook her head. "We stay quiet, we observe, we follow the rules. This is practice. Small steps. It's how my father prepared for everything. Obedience rules, observation techniques, behavioral tests—everything."

They began with simple exercises. Lila instructed Jonah to follow a series of increasingly precise commands: move an object, arrange symbols, respond to cues. Each task seemed mundane, but she observed carefully: timing, hesitation, micro-expressions.

"Notice your response," Lila said as Jonah picked up a pen. "Every action you take is being observed—even in simulation. The organization counts every second, every motion. This is about awareness."

Next, they practiced subtle influence. Lila left a note in Jonah's notebook: *Place this on the windowsill at 8:00 PM.* She watched as he complied exactly, without hesitation, internalizing the principle that obedience could be observed and measured—even between allies.

Afterward, she reversed roles. Jonah issued instructions, and Lila obeyed meticulously, noting her own reactions. "Obedience isn't about blind following," she whispered. "It's about learning patterns, understanding consequences, and testing limits safely."

Hours passed. They experimented with codes, signals, and subtle observation techniques. Every minor success reinforced their understanding of how influence and compliance worked. Every mistake revealed vulnerabilities—both in their approach and in themselves.

By nightfall, Lila's notebook was filled with diagrams, observations, and personal reflections. "This is only the beginning," she said. "We need to understand rules, limits, and reactions before we step into the field. One slip, one wrong move, and the organization will notice."

Jonah nodded, determination replacing his earlier hesitation. "I get it now. It's more than following instructions—it's thinking ahead, anticipating responses, controlling what's visible."

Lila pressed the book to her chest. "Exactly. Knowledge is power. Obedience is survival. And when we're ready, we'll test them in the real world."

Outside, shadows shifted in the dim moonlight, but inside the attic, a small spark of strategy, trust, and readiness had been lit. Lila knew the training wasn't just preparation—it was their first step toward surviving the organization's labyrinth and turning its rules to their advantage.

Chapter 24: First Mission to Gather Information

The night air was thick with anticipation as Lila and Jonah crouched behind the chain-link fence surrounding the abandoned warehouse. The building had been marked in her father's notes as a minor hub for the organization—an operations site, but not heavily monitored. Perfect for a first mission.

"Are you sure we should be here?" Jonah whispered, fidgeting with the strap of his backpack.

Lila's eyes scanned the shadows. "We've trained for this. Stick to the rules, observe, record, and don't draw attention. We're here to gather information, nothing more."

They slipped through a side gate, careful to avoid the weakly patrolled entrances. Lila pulled the book from her backpack, flipping to her annotated diagrams of behavioral patterns. "Watch their movements. Note communication patterns. Every glance, every gesture could reveal hierarchy or hidden messages."

Inside, dim light flickered from a single overhead lamp. Two figures moved in a coordinated rhythm, flipping through documents, tapping on tablets, whispering instructions. Lila's heart raced. Each movement matched the subtle patterns her father had outlined in the Code.

Jonah whispered, "This is... intense."

"Focus," Lila said. "Record everything. Obey the principles: blend in, observe, and never engage unless necessary."

They moved silently to a corner, jotting observations and sketching layouts in their notebooks. Lila noticed a series of coded signals between the two operators—hand gestures, subtle nods, and objects moved in precise patterns. She quickly copied them, realizing these were minor obedience rules in action, enforcing behavior without overt commands.

Suddenly, a metallic clang echoed through the room. Lila froze. A shadow passed the doorway. The two enforcers—stern, imposing figures—glanced briefly toward them but didn't notice. Lila's heart pounded in her chest. Every second was a test. Every movement could expose them.

She held her breath, signaling Jonah to stay low. Slowly, the enforcers moved on, their presence a stark reminder of the danger surrounding even minor hubs.

Once the room was clear, Lila whispered, "We have what we need. Time to exit quietly." They retraced their path, every step calculated, until they slipped back into the night air.

Breathless, Jonah asked, "Do you think they noticed us at all?"

Lila shook her head. "Not yet. But we learned something invaluable tonight: patterns, hierarchy, influence methods. This is the first real step. The Code isn't just theory—it works in practice. And now we have our first intelligence to build on."

As they walked home under the moonlight, shadows lingering at the edge of the streets, Lila realized that the world her father had warned her about was larger, more complex, and far more dangerous than she had imagined. But for the first time, she felt a measure of control. They were no longer just observers—they were participants in the game.

Chapter 25: A Near-Fatal Encounter with Enforcers

The alley behind the warehouse smelled of damp concrete and rust. Lila and Jonah moved cautiously, carrying the notes and sketches they had gathered during their first mission. Every sound echoed unnaturally in the night, and every shadow seemed alive.

"Did we... did we really get everything?" Jonah whispered, his voice trembling.

"For now," Lila replied, scanning the street. "But keep your eyes open. They could follow us."

As if on cue, two dark figures emerged from the shadows at the far end of the alley—enforcers. Tall, imposing, and silent, their presence radiated authority and danger.

Lila's pulse spiked. *Stay calm. Observe. Apply the Code.* She pressed the book closer in her mind, recalling her father's notes on evasion and subtle influence.

The enforcers advanced slowly, scanning the alley. Lila and Jonah ducked behind a dumpster, hearts pounding. One enforcer paused, pointing directly in their direction, though it seemed uncertain.

"Don't move," Lila whispered to Jonah. She mimicked a confident posture, recalling the minor obedience rules: projecting authority without confrontation. Slowly, she slid sideways, dragging Jonah with her behind a stack of crates.

The enforcer's gaze lingered for a moment, then shifted toward another sound—the distant clatter of trash bins. They moved off, but not without leaving a chilling warning: a folded note at the edge of the alley, reading simply: *Obey, or consequences follow.*

Jonah exhaled shakily. "That... was close."

Lila nodded, adrenaline coursing through her veins. "Too close. But it proves something important: even minor exposure can be deadly. Observation is key, but timing and subtlety matter more than anything."

Once safe, they ducked into a nearby doorway to regroup. Lila pulled out her notebook and scribbled furiously: *Lesson: Enforcers enforce fear, observe constantly. Misstep or hesitation could be fatal. Disguise confidence. Blend in. Move strategically.*

Jonah looked up, pale but determined. "So... we're really in this now. There's no turning back."

Lila's eyes hardened. "No turning back. And we'll need to be smarter, faster, and more careful than ever. The Code is our only advantage. Every move must count."

Outside, the alley was silent again, but the memory of the enforcers' presence lingered like a shadow at the back of their minds. The first real test of survival had arrived—and both Lila and Jonah understood that the organization's reach and ruthlessness were far greater than they had imagined.

Chapter 26: Learning the Organization's Hierarchy

The dim glow of Lila's desk lamp illuminated stacks of notes, sketches, and diagrams. After their near-fatal encounter with the enforcers, Lila knew that survival depended on understanding not just behavior, but the entire structure of the organization.

Jonah leaned over the sketches, pointing at a series of symbols. "So these people we saw in the warehouse—are they just low-level workers?"

"Exactly," Lila said. "We saw the enforcers and the operators handling documents. They follow orders, enforce rules, and report irregularities. But the real decisions happen higher up."

She spread her notes across the table. Charts from her father's book showed multiple layers: enforcers at the bottom, then mid-level council members, coordinators overseeing multiple cells, and the hidden leadership—those who dictated the Code itself.

"Look at this," Lila continued, tracing a line from the enforcers up to a symbol she hadn't fully decoded. "I think this represents someone—or something—known as the Master Code. They're at the top, unseen but controlling every rule, every punishment, every movement."

Jonah frowned. "So the enforcers we almost ran into... they're just tools. The real power is invisible."

"Yes," Lila replied. "And every level has its own rules. Compliance, influence, punishment. It's a chain of control. If we understand it, we can predict reactions, manipulate outcomes, and avoid detection—but we have to be precise."

She paused, her pen hovering over the diagram. "Our mission isn't just gathering intel anymore. We need to map the hierarchy completely. Every rank, every code, every pattern of behavior. Knowledge is power. Observation is survival."

Jonah nodded, determination replacing fear. "Step by step. We gather, we observe, we analyze. And then...?"

"Then," Lila said, pressing the book to her chest, "we exploit what we know. But carefully. One misstep could cost us everything."

As they worked late into the night, tracing lines, decoding symbols, and connecting observations from their first mission, Lila realized the scale of the challenge. The organization wasn't just a shadowy group—it was a system. And understanding its hierarchy was the key to dismantling it, surviving it, and eventually using the Code to their advantage.

Outside, the shadows seemed less threatening than before—not because danger had vanished, but because knowledge gave them an edge. And Lila understood, more clearly than ever, that survival meant learning the rules, predicting actions, and preparing for every contingency.

Chapter 27: Ethical Dilemma – Betray Someone to Gain Trust

The quiet hum of the attic felt heavier than usual. Lila stared at her notebook, tracing connections in the organization's hierarchy. Jonah sat nearby, flipping through his own notes, unaware of the storm brewing in Lila's mind.

"There's a new test," Lila said finally, her voice low. "We need access to one of the mid-level council members. They control operations for the small cells in town. If we get their trust, we can gather far more intel."

Jonah frowned. "And how do we do that?"

Lila hesitated. Her father's notes whispered in her mind: *Obedience requires leverage. Influence requires choice. Trust must be earned—even when it demands compromise.*

"There's someone in the council I know—someone weak, cautious. To gain trust, we'll need to... betray them in a minor way. Expose a secret they've been hiding."

Jonah's eyes widened. "Betray... someone? Even a little? That's crossing a line."

Lila nodded grimly. "I know. But the organization doesn't play by moral rules. If we want to survive, we have to operate in their game. Our actions have consequences, but calculated risk can save lives in the long run."

They spent the night planning. Every move, every message, every small act of betrayal had to be precise. Lila rehearsed how she would approach the council member, carefully framing the revelation as helpful, not threatening, to avoid suspicion while demonstrating loyalty.

The next day, Lila executed the plan. She subtly exposed a minor infraction—a misfiled report—and suggested a corrective measure that would align with council expectations. The council member's eyes narrowed but didn't suspect her involvement. Instead, they saw her as competent, observant, and reliable.

Jonah whispered afterward, "You... did it. You betrayed someone and got what we needed."

Lila felt a knot in her stomach. "Yes. And I hate that it worked. But this is the Code in practice—observe, influence, survive. Every choice has a price, Jonah. We just have to decide if the cost is worth it."

That night, Lila journaled her reflection: *Lesson: Morality is tested in the shadows. Obedience and betrayal coexist. Strategic decisions may conflict with personal ethics. Survival demands difficult choices.*

As she closed her notebook, shadows outside the window seemed longer, darker. Lila realized that understanding the Code wasn't just about observation or influence—it was about reconciling her conscience with the ruthlessness the world demanded. And the harder choices were yet to come.

Chapter 28: Decoding a Hidden Message from Her Father

Lila sat at her desk, the dim glow of her lamp illuminating the pages of *The Obedience Code*. Her fingers traced a margin note she hadn't fully understood before: a series of symbols, seemingly random, but familiar from the diagrams she had studied in recent weeks.

Father... what were you trying to tell me? she whispered, leaning closer.

She flipped open her father's old journal, searching for patterns. On page 73, she found a coded message, scribbled hastily:

"Obedience is a tool; morality is a compass. Observe every shadow. Trust cautiously. The path forward is in the minor rules—they reveal the major truths."

Lila's pulse quickened. Her father had left her not just a set of instructions, but a philosophy—a guide for navigating the dangerous web of obedience and influence.

Jonah leaned over her shoulder. "So... he knew we'd have to make hard choices?"

"Yes," Lila replied, decoding the next line. The symbols translated into coordinates and times—points where minor rules were being tested in real life. "He's showing us how the organization monitors behavior... how they apply rules to control people. If we understand the tests, we can anticipate them, even manipulate outcomes."

They spent hours decoding each section, cross-referencing with notes from their first missions and the hierarchy charts. Every symbol revealed a subtle truth about influence, observation, and control.

Lila paused, reflecting on the ethical dilemma from the previous chapter. *Father's guidance... it's not about avoiding moral compromises—it's about using knowledge wisely to survive while preserving core principles.*

Jonah broke the silence. "It's like he left us a map... and a moral compass at the same time."

Lila nodded. "Exactly. Every rule, every observation, every choice has consequences. But now we can navigate them intentionally, rather than blindly reacting."

As she closed the journal, a sense of clarity settled over her. The organization was vast, dangerous, and ruthless—but her father had given her tools, insight, and a framework. And with careful application, she could survive, influence outcomes, and maybe even dismantle the system from within.

Outside, shadows crept along the walls, but Lila no longer flinched. The Code was no longer just a set of abstract principles—it was a living guide, a strategy, and a weapon. And she was ready to wield it.

Chapter 29: Witnessing the Organization Punish Disobedience

The night was thick with silence as Lila and Jonah followed the path her father's decoded coordinates had revealed. It led them to a neglected courtyard on the edge of town, where crumbling brick walls concealed the presence of watchers.

"Stay low," Lila whispered, pulling Jonah into the shadow of a broken fountain. "Something's happening here. It's one of the tests."

A small group had gathered under a dim streetlight. Their faces were tense, their postures rigid. At the center stood an enforcer, tall and commanding, his voice sharp like a blade. Before him, a trembling man—middle-aged, ordinary, terrified.

"You disobeyed," the enforcer barked. "The Code was clear: lights out at midnight. You defied the order. Do you deny it?"

The man stammered, "I... I was helping my daughter with her studies—just a few minutes—"

The enforcer raised his hand, silencing him. "Obedience is not conditional. You know the consequence."

Two other enforcers stepped forward, dragging the man to his knees. The crowd watched in silence, fear etched into every face. No one intervened. No one dared.

Jonah's hand tightened on Lila's arm. "We have to stop this."

"No," Lila whispered fiercely, her voice trembling with anger. "We can't. Not now. We observe. Remember the Code—watch, learn, survive."

The punishment was swift and merciless. The man was branded with a symbol on his wrist—a mark of shame, a reminder to others. His cries echoed through the courtyard as he was dragged away. The crowd dispersed quickly, avoiding eye contact, each person retreating into the shadows.

Lila's stomach twisted. Her father's words echoed in her mind: *Obedience is a tool; morality is a compass.* But what good was morality if it meant standing by while innocents suffered?

Jonah's eyes burned with fury. "They destroyed him... for nothing. For a light."

Lila forced herself to breathe. "It wasn't about the light. It was about control. The rule was arbitrary, but the punishment reinforced obedience. Fear is the real law here."

They slipped away unseen, but the image of the man's branded wrist haunted them both. In her notebook later that night, Lila wrote: *Lesson: Disobedience is punished not for the act, but for the defiance. The organization thrives on fear, not justice. To fight it, we must understand fear and wield it carefully.*

As she closed the book, Lila knew the stakes had risen. This wasn't just about observing rules—it was about surviving in a world where even the smallest act of defiance could end a life.

Chapter 30: Lila Questions Her Own Morality

Sleep didn't come easily that night. Every time Lila closed her eyes, she saw the man's face—contorted in fear and pain as the enforcers branded his wrist. His scream lingered in her ears like a haunting echo.

Jonah had stormed off after walking her home, muttering that he couldn't just stand by anymore. Lila had wanted to stop him, to say something that would make sense of what they had witnessed, but her throat had been tight with guilt.

Now, alone in her room, she sat at her desk, the dim glow of her lamp spilling over *The Obedience Code*. Its pages stared back at her like an accusation.

"Was I wrong to do nothing?" she whispered into the silence.

Her father's handwriting in the margins seemed to answer, though no sound filled the room: *Observe before you act. A rushed rebellion is a failed rebellion.*

But what about the man? He hadn't had the luxury of patience. He had suffered because others stayed silent—just as she had.

The window creaked. Lila froze, then turned slowly. For a split second, she thought she saw a shadow withdraw into the night. Her chest tightened. *Were they watching me too?*

A knock startled her. She shoved the book under her journal. "Who is it?"

"It's me." Jonah's voice. Rough, angry.

She let him in. He paced her room, fists clenched. "I can't stop seeing it. That mark. That sound. And we just... hid."

"We couldn't risk exposure," Lila argued, though her words rang hollow even to her. "If we'd interfered, we'd be the ones branded—or worse."

Jonah stopped, eyes blazing. "Then what's the point of this? What's the point of your father's book if we're just going to watch people suffer?"

The question stabbed at her. She had no answer. Not yet.

Finally, she whispered, "The point is to survive long enough to make a difference. If we fall now, everything dies with us. My father's secrets, the truth, any chance to stop them."

Jonah's expression softened, but only slightly. "And what about our humanity? What's left of us if we stay silent every time?"

Lila swallowed hard, tears pricking her eyes. "That's what I'm afraid of. That in fighting them, we'll become like them. Obedience... cruelty... silence. Where's the line between survival and surrender?"

Jonah sank into the chair across from her, his anger collapsing into exhaustion. "Maybe the line doesn't exist anymore."

Lila opened her journal and wrote: *Question: Can silence be as dangerous as obedience?*

When she looked up, she saw Jonah watching her—not with anger this time, but with something heavier. Doubt.

And for the first time since her father's death, Lila wondered if she truly had the strength to carry this fight.

Chapter 31: Betrayal by a Friend

The next morning, Lila walked into school with heavy eyes. Jonah hadn't said much when they parted, but his words still replayed in her head. The line between survival and surrender.

As she crossed the hallway, she spotted **Mara**, her closest friend since childhood, leaning against a locker. For a moment, relief swept over her. Mara had always been her safe place, the one person untouched by the shadows of The Obedience Code.

"Hey," Mara greeted with a bright smile. "Rough night?"

Lila nodded cautiously. "Yeah. Just... couldn't sleep."

Mara tilted her head. "You've been different lately. Distracted. Is something going on?"

The question landed too precisely. Lila's stomach twisted. She forced a laugh. "Just... stress, I guess."

Mara's smile faltered, then returned. "You know you can trust me, right?"

But the words didn't feel comforting. They felt rehearsed.

Later that afternoon, during free period, Lila ducked into the library to check the encrypted flash drive her father had left behind. She had hidden it inside a hollowed-out textbook. Heart racing, she slid the drive into the computer.

The screen flickered—then froze. A warning message appeared in bold red letters:

"Access denied. Unauthorized attempt logged."

Panic surged. Someone had tampered with it.

She heard a shuffle behind her. Whipping around, she saw Mara standing at the edge of the stacks.

"Mara? What are you doing here?"

Mara's eyes dropped to the flash drive. "You should've told me, Lila. About your father. About the book."

The words knocked the air out of her. "How do you—"

Mara stepped closer, lowering her voice. "They know, Lila. They've been watching you. They told me to look after you. To... report if you were acting strange."

It felt like the floor dropped out from under her. "You're... one of them?"

Mara's face crumpled. "I didn't want to. But they said if I didn't, they'd come for my family. You don't understand—"

Lila backed away, the betrayal cutting sharper than any blade. "I trusted you."

"Please," Mara whispered, reaching out. "I was trying to protect you."

The sound of footsteps echoed in the hallway outside. Heavy, deliberate. Enforcers.

Lila's chest tightened. She grabbed the flash drive, shoved it into her pocket, and bolted toward the back exit. Mara's voice followed her:

"Lila, wait! You don't know what you're up against!"

But Lila didn't stop. Her only thought as she sprinted into the cold air: *Even my friends aren't safe. I can trust no one.*

Chapter 32: Escaping a Trap Using Her Wits

The cold air bit at Lila's skin as she sprinted down the alley behind the school. The pounding of boots echoed closer with every second. Enforcers.

Her heart hammered. *Think, Lila. Think.*

She darted left toward the marketplace, weaving between carts and startled shoppers. People glanced at her, then quickly looked away—fear of involvement etched into their expressions. The crowd parted instinctively, as if trained not to obstruct an enforcer's hunt.

The heavy steps grew louder. She could almost feel their breath at her neck.

Spotting a narrow passage between two old buildings, she ducked inside. The alley dead-ended with a locked iron gate. Panic surged. Trapped.

She pressed her palms against the cold bars, searching for an opening, a weakness—anything. Then she remembered the strange *rule* she'd tested from her father's book: *Authority can be redirected by suggestion when urgency is convincingly displayed.*

Lila crouched low, smeared dirt across her face, and began to tremble deliberately. She whispered to herself, *Play the part.*

When the first enforcer rounded the corner, she collapsed against the gate, clutching her chest. "Please—help me! There's a man—down the other street—he collapsed! You have to hurry!"

The enforcer hesitated, eyes narrowing behind his mask. Seconds stretched into eternity.

Then another enforcer appeared, impatient. "What's wrong?"

"She says someone's down," the first muttered.

Lila seized the moment. "He was foaming at the mouth—something's wrong! Hurry, please!" Her voice cracked, desperation raw.

The second enforcer cursed under his breath. "Fine. Check it out."

Both turned and sprinted back the way she had pointed.

Lila didn't breathe until their footsteps faded. Quickly, she scanned the gate again. Her fingers found a loose hinge hidden in the rust. With a grunt, she yanked it free just enough to slip through the narrow opening.

On the other side, she collapsed against the wall, heart pounding, sweat slicking her palms.

She had escaped—not through strength, but through wit.

As she caught her breath, the flash drive in her pocket pressed against her side like a burning reminder. Mara's betrayal. The Code's strange rules working in real time.

And the chilling truth: *If she could manipulate them, the organization could just as easily manipulate her.*

Chapter 33: Discovering a Traitor Inside Her Inner Circle

Lila didn't stop moving until she reached the abandoned greenhouse on the edge of town—their makeshift hideout. Its glass panes were cracked, ivy curling around the frames, but it was quiet and hidden, a place that had always felt safe.

Inside, Jonah was pacing, muttering under his breath. Two other allies, **Kira** and **Samir**, sat at a rickety wooden table, whispering over a map spread with red markers.

The moment Lila entered, Jonah froze. Relief flickered across his face. "Where were you? We thought you'd been taken."

"I almost was," she said, pulling the flash drive from her pocket. Her hands shook, but her voice was steady. "Someone tipped them off. They knew where I'd be."

The greenhouse went still. All eyes turned toward her.

"Who?" Kira asked sharply.

Lila's throat tightened. She glanced at Jonah—his expression unreadable—then at Kira, then Samir. The memory of Mara's confession burned. But Mara wasn't the only one who knew things.

"I don't know yet," Lila admitted. "But someone's feeding them information. Someone close."

Samir leaned back, crossing his arms. "That's a serious accusation. You can't just throw suspicion without proof."

Jonah's jaw tightened. "She doesn't need proof. We all know something's wrong. Every time we make a move, they're a step ahead."

The air thickened with suspicion.

Lila pulled a folded page from her journal. It was a note she had found slipped under her bedroom door the night before:

"Beware the one who smiles while you suffer."

She laid it on the table. "My father left me this clue. He knew someone couldn't be trusted."

Kira frowned, her eyes flicking between Lila and the note. "That's vague. It could mean anyone."

Jonah stepped closer to Lila, lowering his voice. "Who do you think it is?"

She hesitated. Her gut screamed not to say it aloud, but the tension demanded an answer. Finally, she whispered, "Samir."

Samir shot to his feet, anger flashing. "That's ridiculous! I've risked everything to be here."

"Then explain this," Jonah snapped, holding up a crumpled slip of paper he'd pulled from his jacket. It was a message written in coded shorthand—the same kind her father used in *The Obedience Code.*

Samir's face went pale. "Where did you get that?"

"It was hidden in your bag," Jonah growled.

Silence hung heavy. Kira's hand drifted toward the knife at her belt.

Samir's voice cracked. "I didn't betray you! They already knew things—if I didn't give them something small, they would've killed my brother. You don't understand!"

Lila's chest clenched. *Another betrayal. Another pawn in their game of control.*

Jonah's eyes were fire. "You put us all at risk."

Lila raised a hand, her voice firm. "Stop. If we tear each other apart, they've already won."

But inside, she knew the damage was done. Their circle was fractured, and the shadows were closing in.

Chapter 34: Tension with Allies Over Strategy

The greenhouse no longer felt like a sanctuary. It felt like a cage filled with snapping teeth.

Kira slammed her knife into the table, the blade quivering in the wood. "We can't keep carrying dead weight. Samir's compromised. Cut him loose before he drags us all down."

Samir bristled. "Easy for you to say when you've got no one to protect! They threatened my brother. What was I supposed to do—let him die?"

"That's exactly what they want," Jonah shot back, fists clenched. "They dangle family, friends, anyone they can use. If we all start making exceptions, we're done."

Lila stood at the center, feeling the group tear at its seams. Her father's book weighed heavily in her satchel, as though demanding she assert control. But what authority did she have left?

"We can't afford to lose focus," she said, voice shaking but determined. "Our enemy isn't each other—it's the organization. They thrive on mistrust. Every second we fight among ourselves, they win."

Kira's glare didn't soften. "Then what's your plan, Lila? Keep Samir in the circle and hope he doesn't sell us out again?"

"I didn't *sell* you out!" Samir snapped, slamming his hands on the table. "I gave them scraps. Lies. Enough to keep them off our trail."

Jonah scoffed. "And how long before scraps aren't enough?"

The air thickened with heat and resentment. The sound of rain against the cracked glass above only sharpened the silence that followed.

Lila drew in a deep breath. "Here's what we'll do. Samir stays—for now. But he'll share every detail of his contact with them. No secrets. No half-truths. If he lies again, I'll be the first to turn him over."

Samir's eyes widened. "Lila—"

She cut him off with a sharp glare. "This isn't mercy. It's strategy. If they think they still have a leash on him, we can use it to feed them false leads. But one wrong move, Samir, and you're done."

Jonah frowned but nodded slowly. "It's risky."

Kira growled under her breath but pulled her knife free from the table. "Fine. But if he slips, his blood's on your hands, Lila."

The tension simmered but didn't break.

Later, when the others had gone, Jonah lingered. He studied her with tired eyes. "You're starting to sound like them."

The words cut deep.

Lila whispered back, almost to herself, "Or maybe I'm just starting to learn how to beat them."

Chapter 35: First Real Success in Subverting Minor Rules

For days after the greenhouse confrontation, the group moved like strangers sharing the same room—close in space but far in trust. Every word was measured, every glance suspicious.

Lila knew she had to give them something, a victory—however small. Something to remind them they weren't just running and fracturing, but fighting back.

She flipped through *The Obedience Code* late one night, tracing her father's handwritten notes in the margins. A particular law caught her eye:

"Rule of Passage: A crowd obeys the first command spoken with authority, regardless of its origin."

Her father's note beneath it read: *Even obedience has loopholes. Test carefully.*

The next day, Lila led Jonah, Kira, and Samir into town under the guise of "testing a lead." The marketplace bustled with people, vendors shouting, enforcers scanning from the edges like vultures.

When a bell clanged, signaling the daily curfew announcement, the crowd began to shuffle toward the central square. An enforcer mounted a platform, barking orders: "All citizens, line up for inspection."

Fear rippled across the people. Obedience fell over them like a net.

Lila's pulse raced. *Now or never.*

She stepped onto a crate, raised her chin, and shouted: "Inspection canceled! Proceed to your homes immediately!"

Her voice cracked slightly—but it carried. Heads turned. For a heartbeat, the crowd froze, uncertain. Then, astonishingly, they obeyed. People began dispersing, hurrying away.

The enforcer bellowed, "Stop! Return to order!" But the moment had shifted. Confusion spread. His authority was no longer absolute.

Jonah grabbed Lila's arm. "It's working. Keep going!"

She raised her voice again, louder this time, forcing confidence into every syllable. "No need for inspection today. Return home!"

The crowd surged outward, scattering before the enforcers could corral them.

One enforcer leapt down, shoving through the chaos, eyes narrowing at Lila—but before he could seize her, Jonah pulled her into an alley. Kira and Samir were right behind, their faces alight with disbelief.

When they finally stopped running, Kira actually laughed—a sharp, wild sound. "You... you just made an entire crowd disobey them."

Samir shook his head, half in awe. "That wasn't supposed to be possible."

Lila's chest heaved, adrenaline still coursing through her veins. She pressed a hand over her satchel, where *The Obedience Code* rested.

Her father's book wasn't just theory. It was a weapon.

For the first time, Lila felt a spark of hope. Maybe they could chip away at the system, one rule at a time.

But deep inside, another truth whispered: *If she could command obedience so easily, how long before she lost herself in the power of it?*

Chapter 36: Growing Paranoia

The victory in the marketplace should have lifted them. Instead, it only made the shadows feel heavier.

For the first time in weeks, the group had proof they could bend the rules, turn obedience back on its masters. Yet every face in the greenhouse wore unease.

"What if someone recognized us?" Kira muttered, pacing in tight circles. "We stood out. Too much attention, too soon."

Samir hunched at the table, his fingers drumming nervously. "They'll tighten their grip. We gave them a reason to look harder. The organization doesn't tolerate public disruption."

Lila tried to project calm, but her hands trembled as she flipped open *The Obedience Code*. Her father's notes glared back: *The first success is always the most dangerous. It breeds confidence and carelessness.*

Confidence, yes. Carelessness... she wasn't so sure. But why did her chest ache every time she thought about how the crowd had obeyed her instead of the enforcers?

Jonah caught her staring into space. "You're worried," he said softly, but it wasn't a question.

She nodded, whispering, "What if it wasn't just luck? What if I'm... changing?"

Before Jonah could answer, a loud *crack* echoed from the greenhouse roof. Everyone froze. Ivy trembled, glass rattled.

Kira snatched her knife. "We're being watched."

Samir bolted toward the door, peering through a sliver in the boards. His voice dropped to a whisper. "There's someone outside. Just... standing there."

Lila's pulse spiked. She crept to the window and risked a glance. A figure in a dark coat lingered by the tree line. Too still. Too deliberate.

"They know," she breathed. "They're closing in."

Kira hissed, "We should move. Now."

But Jonah grabbed Lila's shoulder. "Running every time will tear us apart. We need to think. Maybe it's just paranoia—"

"Or maybe paranoia is what keeps us alive," Lila snapped, harsher than she intended.

The words hung heavy.

That night, long after the others slept, Lila lay awake with *The Obedience Code* open on her lap. Every creak of the greenhouse, every gust of wind outside, made her jolt.

The victory had proven the Code worked—but it also made them visible. And the more she thought about it, the more she felt like a spider in a web she couldn't see, tugged from every direction.

Chapter 37: Lila Learns the Organization Monitors Digital Activity

Morning light spilled through the broken panes of the greenhouse, but it did little to ease the tension that clung to them like fog.

Samir had brought an old laptop, scavenged from his uncle's repair shop. "If your father left hidden files," he said, "they might connect us to others resisting the organization. But we need to dig carefully."

The others gathered around as he booted it up. The screen flickered to life with a grinding whirr. Lila slid the flash drive into the port, heart hammering.

For a moment, the familiar directory appeared: encrypted folders, unreadable without the right codes. Then the laptop froze. A small, white box appeared on the screen.

"Unauthorized device detected. Location logged."

Everyone stiffened.

"What does that mean?" Kira demanded, already reaching for her knife as though she could stab the danger away.

Samir's face went pale. "It means they're watching. Not just files. Every keystroke, every connection, every device. They're tracing us right now."

Jonah slammed the laptop shut, but the damage was done. A sick silence filled the greenhouse.

Lila pulled *The Obedience Code* from her satchel, flipping through the pages until she found what she dreaded: a chapter scrawled in her father's hand—*The Digital Chain*.

Her father's notes:

Obedience no longer requires chains of iron. The chain is information. Once linked, there is no escape without erasure.

Her hands trembled. "They don't just monitor the streets. They monitor *us*. Every signal, every screen."

Jonah's jaw tightened. "So what do we do? Smash every computer, every phone? We can't fight them if we can't communicate."

Samir rubbed his temples. "We need a shadow system—something they can't trace."

Kira scoffed. "And where exactly do we find that? In your uncle's junk pile?"

But Lila wasn't listening. She stared at the words in the Code, a chill spreading down her spine.

Her father had known. He'd known the organization's reach was deeper than anyone suspected.

And now they were marked.

From somewhere far off, a siren wailed, low and haunting. The sound carried across town like a warning bell.

Lila whispered, "They're already coming."

Chapter 38: A Coded Meeting with Her Father's Old Contacts

The greenhouse no longer felt safe. After the laptop incident, every rustle outside and every flicker of light made Lila's chest tighten. The group scattered for the night, but she carried her father's book home tucked beneath her jacket, as if the thin leather could shield her from the invisible net that now surrounded her.

That night, she found another folded slip between the book's pages. The handwriting was unmistakably her father's—sharp, precise, deliberate.

"Seek the ones who met me under the lantern light. Ask not for names. Ask for silence."

Below the words was a symbol: three intersecting circles, one shaded darker than the others.

Lila recognized it. Not from memory, but from instinct—like something her father had taught her without words.

The next day, she walked the backstreets of town. The autumn air was damp, carrying the metallic tang of rain. She stopped at the old clock tower, where a faded poster clung stubbornly to the bricks. On the corner of the poster, barely visible, was the symbol.

A man leaned against the wall nearby, coat collar pulled high. His eyes flicked toward her, then away. Another woman passed, setting a single coin on the fountain's edge. Three intersecting circles were scratched into its surface.

Lila swallowed hard. This was the test.

"I'm here for silence," she said softly.

The man's expression barely changed, but his voice was low and careful. "Then silence you shall keep. Follow."

He led her through twisting alleys, always glancing over his shoulder. Finally, they slipped into a forgotten bookstore, the kind that smelled of dust and moth-eaten pages. The shutters were closed, and a lantern burned low on the counter.

Inside waited three figures, their faces half-hidden in shadow. One wore a silver chain with the circle symbol.

"You are his daughter," the woman with the chain said. Her tone was not a question.

Lila clutched the book tighter. "He left me this. He left me warnings. But I need to know what it all means."

The woman leaned forward, eyes sharp. "Then you've already put yourself in danger. The Code is not just a book—it's a map. A living weapon. And if you carry it, the organization will never stop hunting you."

Lila's throat tightened. "He wanted me to find you. Why?"

The man beside the woman exchanged a glance with her before speaking. "Because he knew one day the chains would tighten. And only those who learn to read between the rules can break them."

The lantern flame guttered as if in agreement. For the first time, Lila felt the weight of her father's legacy not as a burden, but as a torch he had passed to her.

But she also knew: once she accepted it, there would be no turning back.

Chapter 39: Facing the Consequences of a Failed Rebellion Attempt

The alley smelled of smoke and damp earth. Lila crouched behind a stack of crates, her father's book pressed against her chest, eyes fixed on the central square.

A small group of townspeople had gathered earlier that day, emboldened by rumors of Lila's earlier success at subverting the organization's rules. They had attempted a minor rebellion—blocking the enforcer's patrol and defying curfew orders.

Now, the price for their courage became heartbreakingly clear.

From her hiding spot, Lila saw the enforcers descend with ruthless precision. They moved like predators, corners of the square sealed off, exits blocked. The rebels, caught off guard, attempted to flee. Screams echoed, silenced almost instantly by threats, strikes, and the chilling efficiency of the enforcers.

Kira's voice cracked in Lila's ear. "We can't just stand here!"

Lila shook her head. "No. We can't intervene—this isn't our fight yet. Not openly. We observe. We learn. *We survive.*"

Even as she said the words, guilt gnawed at her. One man fell to his knees, pleading for mercy as the enforcers dragged him forward. His family watched from the shadows, powerless.

Jonah muttered under his breath, anger and fear intermingling. "This is what happens when people defy them. Fear... it's the law they live by."

Lila's eyes scanned the scene, absorbing every detail: the enforcers' methods, their order of attack, the patterns in how they punished public dissent. She scribbled notes into her journal, trying to turn horror into strategy.

After the last victim was dragged away, silence fell over the square. The rebellion had been crushed within minutes.

Lila whispered, almost to herself, "Lesson learned. Open defiance is deadly. Subversion must be subtle. Every move must be calculated."

Kira's hand found hers, gripping tightly. "We can't wait too long. The longer we hide, the more they control everything."

Lila looked at her allies—tired, tense, fearful. Her father's book seemed to pulse with significance in her hands. *The Code is dangerous. Survival demands patience and cunning.*

And for the first time, Lila fully understood that every choice, no matter how small, carried the weight of life and death.

Chapter 40: First Hint of a Mysterious "Master Code"

The aftermath of the failed rebellion weighed heavily on Lila. The streets were quieter than usual, the air thick with fear. The marketplace where she had tested *The Rule of Passage* days ago now lay empty, its vendors shuttered, their faces pale with obedience.

In the greenhouse, Lila opened *The Obedience Code* again, searching for answers. Her father's notes had always hinted at something larger—something beyond the rules she had been learning.

A small piece of folded parchment fell from between the pages. On it, written in a precise, looping hand, were three words that made her breath catch:

"Seek the Master Code."

Beneath the words, a symbol she had never seen before—a triangle encircled by a ring of dots—was etched in dark ink.

Jonah peered over her shoulder. "Master Code? What's that supposed to mean?"

Lila traced the symbol with her finger. "I don't know... but if my father left this here, it must be important. Something above the minor rules, the hidden laws... something that controls the whole system."

Kira leaned closer, eyebrows knitted. "You mean... like the brain of the organization?"

"Exactly," Lila said, her voice low but steady. "If we find it, maybe we can understand how everything connects. How they maintain control over every person, every action, every obedience test."

Samir frowned, unease flickering in his eyes. "Sounds dangerous. Whoever created it—whoever holds it—they're untouchable."

Lila's fingers tightened around the parchment. "Then that's why we need it. If we can decode the Master Code, we might finally have leverage. Not just to survive, but to fight back."

Jonah glanced at her, concern shadowing his features. "And if it's a trap?"

She met his gaze, determination hardening in her eyes. "Then we'll survive it. We have to. Everything we've learned, every victory, every mistake—it's all leading us here."

As night fell, Lila stared out the cracked window at the town below. Somewhere, the organization moved like a shadow, unseen but omnipresent. Somewhere, the Master Code waited.

And for the first time since discovering her father's book, Lila felt both the weight of destiny and the spark of hope.

Chapter 41: Reconciling Her Personal Ethics with Survival Tactics

The greenhouse felt suffocating. The flickering lantern cast long shadows across the cracked walls, reflecting the unease twisting inside Lila.

Since the failed rebellion and the discovery of the Master Code, every decision had grown heavier. She wasn't just following rules anymore—she was bending them, testing them, manipulating people.

Jonah watched her silently from the corner, arms crossed. "You've changed," he said finally, his voice low. "You're not just learning the Code... you're using it."

Lila's gaze didn't waver. "I have to, Jonah. If we want to survive, if we want to fight, I need to understand how obedience works. The organization thrives on it. I can't afford to act like a moral idealist anymore."

"But at what cost?" Kira asked, stepping closer. Her knife glinted in the lantern light. "We've seen what bending the rules does. One wrong move, and lives are lost."

Lila closed the book in her lap. "I know. I see that. But every time I hesitate, someone else suffers. My father didn't just write this book for theory—he wrote it to survive, to fight. He wanted me to make hard choices, not easy ones."

Samir, sitting quietly, finally spoke. "Do you ever feel... guilty?"

"Every second," Lila admitted. Her voice was barely a whisper. "I manipulate, I deceive, I test people without their knowledge. I justify it as strategy, but sometimes I wonder if I'm becoming like them. The organization. The enforcers."

Jonah took a step forward. "Then maybe we need a rule—our own Code. Something that keeps us human, even while we fight them."

Lila considered this. A personal compass amidst the chaos. Could she survive without losing herself entirely? She opened her journal and wrote:

Survival does not mean surrender. Obedience can be weaponized. Morality must guide, even when fear presses close. The line between victory and compromise is razor-thin.

The group sat in tense silence. Outside, the town slept under the shadow of unseen eyes, but inside, a fragile resolve was forming.

Lila knew the next steps would demand ruthlessness—but she also vowed that her ruthlessness would be tempered with conscience.

For the first time, she felt a measure of control.

Chapter 42: New Ally with Secret Knowledge Joins

The greenhouse was quieter than usual. The storm outside drummed on the broken glass roof, but inside, the tension was heavier than any storm Lila had felt.

A knock sounded at the door. Lila froze, hand instinctively on her father's book. "Who is it?" she called, her voice steady but wary.

A figure stepped inside—a young man in a worn coat, hood shadowing his face. His eyes flicked over the group, lingering on Lila. "I was told this is where I could find her," he said, voice calm but carrying weight.

"Find *her*?" Jonah asked, suspicion clear. "Who are you?"

"My name is Elias," the man said, stepping closer. "I knew your father. I've been... waiting for someone capable of continuing his work."

Lila felt her pulse quicken. "How do you know about my father?"

Elias pulled a folded piece of parchment from his coat, placing it on the table. It was covered in symbols identical to those in *The Obedience Code*, including the newly discovered Master Code triangle.

"He left me instructions," Elias said. "And warnings. He knew the organization wouldn't stop with him. He believed someone had to understand the Master Code—and someone had to survive to use it."

Kira frowned. "And you think that someone is her?"

Elias's gaze met Lila's, unwavering. "Yes. But only if she's willing to learn, to see the patterns, and to act where others would hesitate."

Samir muttered, "Patterns? Hesitate? What are you talking about?"

Elias smiled faintly. "The organization isn't just rules and enforcers. It's a network, a system built on human obedience, fear, and manipulation. Your father's book is a key—a guide to understanding the mechanics. But the Master Code... that is the engine. It is what controls the entire structure."

Lila's hands shook slightly as she opened her father's book and compared the symbols. Her stomach tightened. Everything she had learned so far—the victories, the betrayals, the escapes—was just the surface.

"And you're here to teach me?" she asked, a mix of awe and skepticism in her voice.

Elias nodded. "I can guide you—but only if you're ready to see the organization as it truly is. If not... it will destroy you."

Lila exchanged a glance with Jonah. He nodded subtly. She felt a surge of determination.

"I'm ready," she said.

The storm outside intensified, as if echoing her resolve. With Elias now among them, a new chapter of their fight—and the path toward the Master Code—was beginning.

Chapter 43: Infiltration of a Small Council Meeting

The night air was damp and heavy as Lila, Jonah, Kira, Samir, and their new ally Elias approached the old town hall. Its brick facade was familiar yet foreboding, the glow of lanterns spilling through high, shuttered windows.

"This is it," Elias whispered, checking the map he'd drawn. "A small council meeting. Minor enforcers, mid-tier administrators. Not the top, but enough to reveal patterns. If we're careful, we can glean insight without being detected."

Lila's stomach knotted. Every mission so far had taught her that mistakes were deadly. But she also knew that waiting too long meant letting the organization consolidate power.

They slipped through a side door, shadows melding with shadows. The council chamber smelled of old wood, wax, and the faint tang of ink. Several mid-level enforcers sat at the long, polished table, papers and ledgers spread before them.

Jonah muttered, "They're just talking. This seems... routine."

Elias shook his head. "Routine is deceptive. Watch the dynamics—the minor rules, the hierarchy, the subtle enforcement cues. That's how they maintain control."

Lila crouched behind a tall column, pulling her father's book from her satchel. She silently cross-referenced a diagram of obedience hierarchies with the people before her.

As one of the council members gestured toward a ledger, Elias whispered, "Notice how the assistants obey without question, even when the orders are contradictory. That's the Code in action."

A surge of understanding hit Lila. These weren't just rules—they were **manipulations embedded in behavior**. Patterns repeated across the organization, creating predictability and, ultimately, control.

Suddenly, one of the council members looked directly toward her hiding spot. Lila froze. Heart hammering, she ducked lower, holding her breath. The figure's gaze lingered for a second, then shifted away, distracted by a report.

"They almost saw us," Kira hissed.

Elias placed a hand on Lila's shoulder. "Good. You're learning. Observation is as powerful as action."

They stayed hidden until the council concluded, noting every minor law enforced, every subtle intimidation, and every act of obedience. When they finally slipped back into the rain-slick streets, Lila's mind buzzed with revelation.

The organization was a system—a living mechanism of compliance. And now, she had the beginnings of a blueprint to understand it from within.

Chapter 44: Lila Witnesses an Assassination Attempt

The streets were unusually quiet that evening, the kind of silence that felt heavy and unnatural. Lila and her allies followed Elias's directions carefully, keeping to shadowed alleyways as they approached the location he had identified: a small public forum where a mid-ranking council member was expected to speak.

"This is a perfect observation point," Elias whispered, crouched behind a low wall. "Not too close to risk exposure, but close enough to see the interactions. Watch for enforcement patterns. Watch for anomalies."

Lila squatted beside him, heart pounding in anticipation. She scanned the crowd, noting the way people shifted uneasily when the enforcers passed, the subtle obedience displayed in every gesture.

Then a commotion at the podium caught her attention. One of the council member's guards staggered forward, clutching his chest. Lila froze.

A second figure emerged from the crowd, hand flashing toward the councilman with a small, concealed device. Seconds felt like hours.

Kira gasped. "She's trying to—"

Before Kira could finish, Elias lunged, grabbing Lila and yanking her to the ground. A sharp sound cracked through the air—a gunshot, muffled yet terrifying. People screamed and scattered, some tripping over each other in panic.

Lila's hands shook. "They—someone tried to kill him!" she whispered.

Elias nodded grimly. "Not just anyone. The organization is cleaning house. Internal threats, insubordination, mistakes—they don't tolerate failure. What you saw was a demonstration, and a warning."

Jonah clenched his fists. "We can't just watch them kill people and do nothing!"

Lila swallowed, eyes darting toward the fleeing figure. "We *have* to learn first. Understand the pattern. Every failure, every assassination, every punishment—it's all part of their system. If we react blindly, we'll play right into their hands."

The council member survived, whisked away by backup enforcers, but the message was clear: defiance came at a cost, and even minor players were expendable.

Lila's mind raced as she recorded every detail mentally—the timing, the guards' responses, the reactions of the crowd. Each observation was a piece of the larger puzzle, a piece of the Master Code she was desperate to decode.

As they slipped into the shadows, Elias whispered, "You're learning quickly. But remember, observation is not safety. Never forget that."

Lila nodded, adrenaline still coursing through her veins. Fear had sharpened her instincts. Danger was everywhere—but now, she had a deeper understanding of the organization's ruthlessness.

And she vowed silently: the next time, she would not merely observe.

Chapter 45: Organization's Enforcers Tighten Control

The town felt smaller, constricted, as if the streets themselves were closing in. Lila noticed it immediately—more patrols, more checkpoints, more eyes. The air, once heavy with fear, now carried an oppressive weight of surveillance and order.

"They're reacting," Jonah muttered, scanning the street ahead. "After the assassination attempt, they're cracking down everywhere."

Kira's jaw was tight. "We can't move anywhere without being watched. Every alley, every shop... it's like a trap waiting to spring."

Samir adjusted the hood over his head, glancing nervously at every passerby. "We're small fry. But the message is clear—any one of us could be next."

Lila tightened her grip on her father's book. The lessons she had learned—the rules of obedience, subtle manipulation, observing patterns—were all more vital than ever. Every misstep now could lead to death.

Elias appeared beside her silently, voice low. "They're increasing checkpoints, curfews, and surveillance. Every minor rule enforced is now a test. People are scared to even whisper."

A man stumbled past, nearly colliding with Lila. He muttered something under his breath about missing a curfew and glanced over his shoulder, eyes wide with panic. The enforcers standing nearby didn't flinch—they were the silent embodiment of fear.

Lila's mind raced. "They're controlling more than obedience now—they're controlling movement, speech... even thought. Every action is being monitored. Every reaction recorded."

Jonah shook his head grimly. "We knew it was bad, but this... this is more than we expected."

Lila opened the book, tracing diagrams of minor obedience rules, now realizing how easily they were used to manipulate the town.

"They're teaching fear through discipline, through subtle control, through constant monitoring. Every citizen is a lesson."

Kira's hand brushed Lila's shoulder. "So what do we do? Hide forever?"

Lila looked at her allies, the rain-slicked streets, the tightening grip of the enforcers. "No. We adapt. Every pattern, every rule, every test—they leave cracks. That's where we'll strike. But first, we survive, we observe, and we learn."

Elias nodded silently. "And we prepare. For the next move, they will escalate further. This is only the beginning."

Lila's heart pounded. The organization's control was tightening like a vice—but now, with knowledge, strategy, and patience, she felt a flicker of confidence. Survival was no longer just about hiding. It was about learning the system, bending it, and one day... breaking it.

Chapter 46: Learning Manipulation Tactics on Townspeople

The rain had stopped, leaving the streets glistening under the faint glow of lanterns. Lila walked alongside Elias, Kira, Jonah, and Samir, each step cautious, eyes constantly scanning for enforcers.

"We can't fight them openly," Elias whispered. "Not yet. But we *can* learn to manipulate the population. Not by force, but by guiding their obedience subtly."

Lila's brow furrowed. "Manipulate? Like... trick them?"

Elias shook his head. "Not trick. Influence. People follow patterns—they respond to authority, fear, reward, and social pressure. We'll use minor rules, hints, and cues to create controlled behaviors. Small steps. Minimal risk."

Kira raised an eyebrow. "Sounds like brainwashing."

"Subtle influence," Lila corrected. "Not control—guidance. We create choices that feel free, but we're steering the outcomes."

They chose a small market square where the enforcers' patrols were less frequent. Lila observed the vendors and townspeople: how they obeyed the posted curfew, how fear influenced their gestures, how even small encouragements could sway behavior.

Elias handed her a list of minor obedience rules from her father's book. "Start small," he said. "Observe a pattern, then gently nudge it. Test response, note results, adapt."

Lila took a deep breath. She approached a fruit vendor, holding a small note of instruction under the table. "Place this sign here," she whispered. "Tell customers it's a recommendation from the council."

The vendor hesitated but obeyed. Moments later, other vendors followed, unconsciously mimicking. Foot traffic shifted subtly, patterns of purchase changed. Lila watched as small obedience rippled through the crowd, creating a microcosm of influence.

Jonah leaned close. "It works. But... is it ethical?"

Lila clenched her fists, torn. "Ethics are luxury. Survival is necessity. And if we can sway even a few without bloodshed, we gain advantage."

Samir frowned but nodded. "I see it. This is the kind of power the organization has been using all along. We're learning it for ourselves."

By nightfall, Lila had mapped several behavioral patterns and minor manipulations, each a small victory. But as she watched the town respond—sometimes predictably, sometimes unexpectedly—she knew one thing: every act of influence carried consequences, and the line between survival and manipulation blurred with every decision.

Chapter 47: Discovering the Organization's Global Reach

The greenhouse smelled of damp wood and dust, but tonight it felt electric with tension. Lila sat cross-legged on the floor, *The Obedience Code* open before her, Elias leaning close over her shoulder.

"There's something you need to see," Elias murmured, pulling out a laptop from his coat. "Your father left traces—not just for this town, but hints of a network spanning continents."

Lila's eyes widened. "A network? You mean... the organization isn't just local?"

Elias shook his head. "Far from it. Curfews, rules, obedience protocols—they're replicated globally. Similar patterns, similar enforcers, similar punishments. Your town is just a node."

He typed rapidly, and a map appeared on the screen. Red dots blinked in clusters across multiple continents—Europe, Asia, North America, Africa. Each dot represented a known location of influence, control, and enforcement.

Kira leaned in, voice low. "That's... massive. How can one organization manage that?"

Elias's gaze was steady. "Control doesn't require presence. It requires obedience. Fear and manipulation ripple faster than armies. Rules replicated, behaviors predicted, systems monitored. The organization's reach is algorithmic, human, and invisible."

Lila traced her finger over a cluster in South America. "This... this is insane. How did my father even know about this?"

Elias smiled faintly. "He had contacts, intelligence, networks. He studied obedience patterns the world over. That's why he left *The Obedience Code*—to pass on not just knowledge, but strategy. He knew someone would need to fight back."

Jonah ran a hand over his face. "So everything we've seen... the curfews, the enforcers, the rules—they're all part of a global system?"

"Yes," Elias said firmly. "And every minor victory here could teach them—and us—something. Patterns that repeat. Mistakes we can exploit. But also vulnerabilities we cannot ignore."

Lila leaned back, mind racing. The scale of the fight ahead was overwhelming. Her small acts of rebellion suddenly felt like tiny sparks against a continent-spanning machine.

And yet... she felt a spark of determination. If the organization had built a global web, then understanding it—decoding it—was the first step to dismantling it.

Her father's book was no longer just a guide for survival in one town. It was a blueprint for resistance against something much larger, much more dangerous

Chapter 48: Allies Debate Whether to Expose Secrets

The greenhouse was tense, the lanterns casting jagged shadows across tired faces. Lila, Elias, Jonah, Kira, and Samir sat around a splintered wooden table, the rain pattering against the roof in a steady rhythm.

Elias opened his notebook, revealing diagrams and coded notes. "We've gathered enough information," he said. "The question now is whether to release it. Exposing the organization could ignite rebellion, but it could also trigger catastrophic retaliation."

Kira's eyes flashed. "We *have* to warn people. They can't live in fear forever. If we stay silent, we're complicit."

Jonah shook his head. "You don't understand. One leak, one message—millions could die. The organization is global, and they'll strike ruthlessly. Discretion is our only weapon."

Samir leaned forward. "But silence means waiting indefinitely. Are we supposed to just survive while others suffer? We've seen the consequences—people die every day under their rules."

Lila's hands rested on her father's book, tracing the diagrams of obedience and control. "Exposing secrets isn't just a message," she said softly. "It's an action. Every choice carries consequences. But we also have a duty to use this knowledge—to balance survival with resistance."

Elias nodded. "The risk is massive. Exposure could accelerate enforcement, but containment could allow patterns to be exploited strategically. Timing is everything."

Kira slammed her fist lightly on the table. "So we wait? We just watch people suffer?"

Lila's eyes hardened. "No. We *plan*. Every minor action, every subtle nudge we've learned, every piece of intelligence we've gathered—it's all preparation. When we act, it has to be precise. Too soon, and everyone suffers. Too late, and the opportunity is gone."

Jonah exhaled sharply. "So... patience. Strategy over emotion."

Lila nodded. "Exactly. And we stay united. If we fracture now, the organization will crush us individually before we can fight collectively."

The room fell silent. Rain drummed steadily against the roof, matching the slow, measured pulse of the plan forming in their minds. Exposing the organization was tempting—but survival, understanding, and precision would come first.

And in the shadows, the organization's web stretched farther than they could see, waiting for the moment someone made the wrong move.

Chapter 49: Lila Faces a Moral Test: Obey to Save Someone

The night was thick with fog, curling around the streetlamps like restless spirits. Lila and her allies moved cautiously, winding through alleys to avoid enforcer patrols. Every shadow seemed alive, every sound magnified by fear.

A sudden, panicked cry cut through the mist. Lila froze. "Did you hear that?" she whispered.

Jonah nodded grimly. "Someone's in trouble."

They hurried toward the source and found a young boy, no older than twelve, trapped beneath the watchful gaze of two enforcers. He had broken a minor curfew, and his pleading eyes met theirs as if begging for a miracle.

Kira's hand went to her knife. "We can't—"

"Wait," Lila hissed, studying the situation. She felt the tug of her father's lessons—the Code, the rules, the obedience patterns. The boy's life hung on a single choice.

One enforcer barked orders, demanding the child stand still. The other prepared a device meant to subdue or punish him instantly.

Lila weighed the options. Rescue attempts would draw attention, but obeying—stepping aside—would let innocence be punished for the sake of survival.

Her hands trembled as she slowly stepped forward, speaking quietly to the enforcer in a tone that mimicked authority. "Wait. He is with me. I'll take responsibility."

The enforcer glanced at her, suspicion in his eyes. Lila carefully enacted the minor obedience rules she had memorized—subtle gestures, measured tone, confident posture. The enforcer hesitated, then nodded, allowing the boy to step back.

The fog swallowed them as Lila led the child away. Jonah caught her arm. "That was too close. You just manipulated them."

She nodded, voice shaking. "I had to. If I followed my conscience without using the Code... he'd be gone. Survival and morality collided, and the Code let me navigate it."

Samir muttered, awe and unease mixing in his tone. "It works. But the cost... is it worth it?"

Lila glanced back at the enforcers standing rigidly in the mist, then at the boy's grateful eyes. "It *is* worth it. Sometimes obedience must be weaponized—for good. And sometimes, survival requires bending morality to save lives."

Her heart pounded, a mix of relief, fear, and understanding. The Code was no longer abstract—it was a tool, a responsibility, and a test of conscience.

Chapter 50: Act 2 Midpoint: Lila Uncovers a Major Organizational Secret

The greenhouse was nearly silent, save for the rhythmic tapping of rain against broken panes. Lila sat cross-legged at the table, *The Obedience Code* open before her, Elias beside her, Jonah and Kira leaning in. Samir paced restlessly.

Elias pointed to a diagram in the book—a series of interlocking circles, lines, and arrows. "Your father left hints about the Master Code. But he also embedded an operational blueprint hidden in plain sight. Few have noticed it."

Lila leaned closer, scanning the pages. Symbols aligned with patterns she had seen in town: the council meetings, patrol schedules, obedience tests, even the manipulation experiments she had orchestrated.

"This... this isn't just a book," she whispered. "It's a map. A network. A system that shows how control is maintained from the bottom up and enforced from the top down."

Jonah frowned. "You mean the Master Code isn't just rules—it's like a... control engine?"

Elias nodded. "Exactly. The organization doesn't just punish or reward—they orchestrate behaviors, anticipate resistance, and manipulate loyalty. The Master Code is the algorithm behind obedience. And your father discovered it."

Lila traced her finger along a hidden line of symbols, realizing that minor obedience rules connected to higher-level enforcement patterns. Every seemingly insignificant action reinforced their system—curfews, curbs, gestures, responses—all nodes in a larger network.

Kira exhaled sharply. "So everything we've seen... it's all connected. Every small control feeds into the bigger picture."

"Yes," Lila said, voice barely above a whisper. "And if we understand this, we can predict their moves. We can find weaknesses, exploit cracks, and maybe... dismantle the system from within."

Samir's face was pale. "But knowing this... we're targets. Every observation makes us more dangerous—and them more aware."

Lila nodded, determination hardening her resolve. "I know. But ignorance isn't an option anymore. We've reached the point where knowledge is our weapon. And this—the Master Code blueprint—is the key to survival and resistance."

As the rain fell harder outside, she felt the weight of her father's legacy pressing down—and the clarity of purpose rising. The fight was no longer just about survival. It was about **understanding the machine of control and finding the path to dismantle it**.

This was the turning point. From now on, every step, every choice, every move would be guided by the Master Code—and the dangerous knowledge it represented.

Chapter 51: Reconciling Personal Ethics with Strategic Use of the Master Code

The greenhouse felt colder than usual, despite the storm raging outside. Lila sat at the table, her father's book open, Elias leaning close with a quiet intensity. Jonah, Kira, and Samir were scattered around, tense and alert.

"We've seen the Master Code," Elias said softly. "Now comes the real test: how to use it without losing yourself—or innocent lives."

Lila's fingers traced the lines connecting the symbols, following patterns she had begun to recognize in the town's behavior. "It's powerful," she admitted. "I can manipulate outcomes, predict enforcers' responses, even guide citizens. But... every time I do, I feel like I'm crossing a line."

Kira crossed her arms, frowning. "You're already bending rules. If you use this Master Code strategically, are we just becoming like them?"

Lila swallowed, heart pounding. "Maybe. But we have to make choices. Every step we take has consequences—sometimes life, sometimes death. If we hesitate because of guilt, we fail. If we act recklessly, we harm others. The Code is a tool; morality must guide its use."

Jonah leaned forward, voice low. "So how do we know when it's right?"

Lila exhaled slowly, looking at her allies. "We set rules for ourselves. Every action must be deliberate, measured, and for the greater good. Survival is not enough—we fight, but we fight ethically."

Elias nodded. "Exactly. The organization weaponizes obedience, fear, and manipulation. We will use the same principles—but with conscience. That is our edge."

Samir's eyes flicked nervously between Lila and the book. "And if we slip? If power corrupts us?"

Lila's gaze hardened. "Then we hold each other accountable. We remember why we started, what we're protecting, and the lives depending on us. Strategy without ethics is destruction. Ethics without strategy is weakness. We need both to succeed."

The rain beat harder against the greenhouse roof, drumming like a warning. Lila closed the book for a moment, letting the weight of responsibility settle.

"We have knowledge. We have tools. And now we have clarity," she said. "The Master Code doesn't control us. We control it. And we will decide how to wield it—for survival and for justice."

A hush fell over the group, resolve settling into each of them. In that moment, Lila understood that true power wasn't in obedience or manipulation alone—it was in **choosing how to use it responsibly**.

Chapter 52: A Coded Meeting with Her Father's Old Contacts

The alley smelled of wet stone and smoke, faint traces of burning wood lingering from the previous night's patrols. Lila, Elias, Jonah, Kira, and Samir moved silently, each step measured, eyes scanning for patrols.

Elias paused at a brick wall, tapping three times in a precise rhythm. Lila felt a shiver of recognition—her father had used similar codes to signal meetings. A small panel slid open, revealing a hidden doorway.

Inside, the room was dimly lit. Shadows clung to corners, faces obscured beneath hoods. Lila's heart raced. These were her father's contacts—people who had once worked in the shadows to counter the organization.

One figure stepped forward, voice low but firm. "Lila Sanchez?"

Lila nodded. "Yes. You knew my father?"

A woman inclined her head. "We did. And he trusted you. That is why we are here—to continue his work."

Elias whispered, "Remember, every word here is coded. Treat information as fragile. The organization watches even whispers."

The woman handed Lila a small, folded sheet. On it were symbols and shorthand familiar from *The Obedience Code*. "These are contacts, resources, and safe locations. Your father documented patterns we could only suspect. Now, it's your turn to act."

Jonah peered over her shoulder. "This is... a network. Underground, hidden from everyone. How do we even begin?"

Lila's fingers traced the coded lines. "We begin by understanding. Every safehouse, every ally, every signal is a piece of the puzzle. The organization controls what is visible. We control what is invisible."

Samir frowned. "And the risks?"

"The risks are death, exposure, betrayal," Elias said calmly. "But the reward is survival, intelligence, and leverage. Your father built this network to protect knowledge—and people."

Lila tucked the sheet into her jacket. "Then we honor him by using it wisely. By observing patterns, decoding signals, and acting strategically. We don't just survive—we prepare."

The room fell into silent agreement. Shadows moved, plans formed. In the hidden corners of the town, a quiet resistance stirred, guided by the knowledge her father had left behind—and the courage Lila now carried forward.

Chapter 53: Facing the Consequences of a Failed Rebellion Attempt

The town smelled of damp stone and lingering smoke. Lila and her allies moved cautiously through the streets, now eerily quiet after the recent failed rebellion attempt. Signs of punishment were everywhere—shutters nailed closed, streets swept clean, citizens whispering behind locked doors.

Jonah exhaled sharply. "This... this is worse than I expected. They didn't just punish the rebels—they've changed the town entirely."

Kira nodded, eyes scanning for enforcers. "Fear is more effective than rules. Everyone's watching each other now. Nobody moves without thinking twice."

Lila's fingers tightened around *The Obedience Code*. The Master Code had given them understanding, but this—this was the real consequence of defiance. Every minor rebellion created ripple effects, and the organization had responded with ruthless precision.

Elias crouched beside her. "We predicted patterns of punishment, but this scale... even I underestimated it. The organization is sending a message: obedience is survival. Resistance is annihilation."

A man hurried past, muttering about friends and family who had been "taken for correction." Lila's stomach churned. Every victory had a cost. Every test of obedience carried consequences she couldn't always control.

Samir's voice trembled. "Are we even ready for this? If we act, if we fail... people die."

Lila looked at the group, determination hardening. "We can't stop. Every failed rebellion teaches us something. Patterns, weaknesses, enforcement timing... all of it. We learn, we adapt, and next time, we succeed without unnecessary loss."

Jonah shook his head. "And if we fail again?"

"Then we use what we've learned to survive and strike smarter," Lila said firmly. "The organization thrives on fear. Knowledge is our weapon. And now, more than ever, we understand the stakes."

The streets were silent once more, but Lila's resolve burned brighter. The consequences of failure were dire—but in understanding them, she saw the path forward. Every observation, every minor action, every coded signal would now be measured against survival, morality, and the ultimate goal: dismantling the organization from within.

Chapter 54: First Hint of a Mysterious "Master Code"

The greenhouse was filled with shadows, flickering lanterns casting uneven light over worn furniture and scattered papers. Lila pored over her father's book, cross-referencing symbols she had recently discovered with notes from Elias.

"There's something here," she murmured, pointing to a faint triangular diagram in the margin, nearly erased by time. "I think this... this isn't part of the minor obedience rules. It's something higher."

Elias leaned close, examining the faint lines. "You're right. Few even suspect it exists. Your father referred to it as the *Master Code.* He said it governed everything else—obedience, hierarchy, enforcement... even the organization's predictive patterns."

Jonah frowned. "So all the rules, the patterns we've learned... they're just pieces of a bigger system?"

"Yes," Lila said softly. "Every minor law, every curfew, every behavior reinforcement—it all connects. And this Master Code... it's the engine."

Kira glanced nervously at the others. "If it's the engine, then discovering it is dangerous. They'd kill anyone who gets close."

Lila nodded. "Exactly. But it's also the key. If we can understand it, we can predict their moves, exploit weaknesses, maybe even dismantle their control. It's why my father left hints instead of instructions—he didn't want just anyone using it."

Samir's voice was low. "And we're the ones picking up the pieces. That's... a lot of responsibility."

"It is," Elias agreed. "And a lot of risk. But your father believed in your judgment. The Master Code isn't just rules—it's a test of intellect, ethics, and courage. Only someone capable of balancing strategy and conscience can handle it."

Lila traced the triangular diagram with her fingertip, feeling a surge of resolve. Every minor rule she had learned, every manipulation she had practiced, every risk she had taken—they were all preparation for this moment.

"The organization built a machine of obedience," she whispered. "And now, we're learning to see its blueprint. The Master Code is the key. We just have to decipher it... before it's too late."

Outside, the town slept under the watchful eyes of the enforcers, unaware that someone was beginning to understand the rules that governed their lives—and how to bend them for survival.

Chapter 55: Reconciling Personal Ethics with the Master Code in Action

The greenhouse smelled of damp wood and ink. Lila sat at the table, her father's book open, the triangular Master Code diagram spread before her. Elias leaned close, whispering, "Theory is one thing. Application is where judgment and morality collide."

Lila's eyes scanned the pages. "I know what you mean. We can predict, manipulate, even bend obedience to our will—but every action has consequences. Every person we influence is still a human being."

Kira shook her head. "So what? We just sit here and do nothing while the organization enforces its rules?"

Lila's gaze hardened. "No. But every move has to be calculated. Subtle. Ethical. The Master Code isn't just about control—it's about understanding patterns, predicting outcomes, and acting responsibly."

Jonah frowned. "Responsible? Isn't any manipulation... wrong?"

Elias intervened gently. "It's a tool. And like any tool, it can be used for good or harm. The question is intention and precision. You've already saved lives by bending minor rules. That's the Code in action. Ethical manipulation is possible."

Lila's mind raced. She thought back to the boy she had saved from enforcers, the nudges in the marketplace, the coded communications with her father's contacts. Each action had balanced risk, morality, and survival.

"Then we proceed with caution," Lila said finally. "Every step, every nudge, every small rebellion—guided by the Code, guided by conscience. Observation first, action second. Always measure the impact."

Samir exhaled. "So the Master Code isn't just about defeating the organization—it's about surviving *without becoming them*."

Lila nodded. "Exactly. Knowledge is power. Ethics are the compass. And strategy is the path. Without any of those three, we fail—not just in our mission, but in ourselves."

Elias placed a hand on her shoulder. "You're ready. Start small, apply the Master Code subtly, test responses, observe patterns. Every minor success builds toward dismantling the organization."

As the rain beat softly against the greenhouse roof, Lila felt clarity for the first time. The Master Code wasn't just a weapon—it was a responsibility. And she would wield it with intelligence, courage, and conscience.

Chapter 56: New Ally with Secret Knowledge Joins

The greenhouse felt unusually crowded for the first time in weeks. Lila, Elias, Jonah, Kira, and Samir had gathered around the table, their minds still buzzing from the Master Code revelations.

A shadow fell across the doorway. Lila instinctively reached for her satchel, but Elias raised a hand.

"Wait," he whispered.

A young woman stepped into the dim light. Her dark coat was weathered, and her eyes held a mixture of wariness and confidence. "Lila Sanchez?" she asked, voice steady.

"Yes," Lila replied cautiously. "Who are you?"

"I'm Selene. Your father helped me years ago—provided guidance when I was trying to resist the organization. I've been tracking patterns ever since."

Elias studied her carefully. "We need to know everything, quickly. Can we trust her?"

Selene nodded. "You have the book. You've begun understanding the Master Code. I can help you go further—connect nodes, predict enforcer movements, and decipher communication networks the organization thought were secure."

Kira's brow furrowed. "And the risk? You've been operating alone this whole time. Why join now?"

Selene's gaze softened slightly. "Because the organization is evolving faster than we anticipated. You need more than observation—you need actionable intelligence. And I can provide that. But we have to work together. No secrets."

Lila studied Selene, sensing her honesty. The subtle confidence, the precision in her speech—it reminded her of her father's discipline. "If you're willing to follow our rules, and our ethics," Lila said slowly, "then you're welcome. But we operate by strategy, not impulse."

Selene smiled faintly. "Understood. I don't work recklessly. I work for results. And I've seen what happens when ethics are ignored. That won't be a problem here."

Elias exhaled quietly. "Then it's settled. Selene joins us. Her knowledge will accelerate our understanding of the Master Code—and the organization's weaknesses."

Lila closed the book, a surge of hope flickering in her chest. With Selene's guidance, patterns that had been opaque were now within reach. They were one step closer to dismantling the organization's network—and one step closer to survival.

Chapter 57: Infiltration of a Small Council Meeting

The council building loomed silently at the edge of town, its dark stone façade reflecting the faint glow of lanterns. Lila crouched behind a hedgerow with Selene, Elias, Jonah, Kira, and Samir, every nerve taut.

"This is your first real infiltration," Selene whispered, her voice calm but urgent. "The council meeting is small, but the information inside could shift everything. Watch patterns, note exits, and stay invisible."

Lila nodded, heart pounding. She could feel the weight of her father's teachings and the Master Code pressing on her mind. Every small gesture mattered. Every movement carried consequences.

They slipped through a side entrance Selene had identified, moving like shadows. Inside, the council chamber was austere, lined with officials and a few enforcers. Papers were neatly stacked, pens poised, the room almost sterile in its order.

Jonah's whisper broke the silence. "We shouldn't be here. One wrong move—"

"Observation first," Lila cut in, her voice steady despite her racing heart. "Action second. Remember the Master Code."

She scanned the council members, noting subtle signs: the hierarchy of attention, body language that betrayed influence, and minor signals indicating subordination. Each detail was a piece of the puzzle.

Selene pointed subtly to a corner. "That clerk over there—he's an informant. Watch him. He controls information flow to the enforcers."

Minutes stretched as Lila and her team absorbed patterns and interactions, mentally recording who held power and how obedience was enforced. Then came the critical moment: one council member reached for a confidential folder, unaware that Lila's small recording device captured the contents.

Kira whispered, "This is it. The proof of manipulation."

Lila's eyes sparkled with determination. "Exactly. And with this, we know how they maintain control over even small council decisions. Patterns repeat. Obedience can be predicted. And once we understand, it can be disrupted."

They retraced their steps silently, exiting through the same hidden passage. Outside, the rain had begun again, drumming softly against the cobblestones. Lila held the device tightly, knowing that what they had captured could be a turning point in their fight against the organization.

This infiltration wasn't just observation—it was the first step toward dismantling the system from within. And Lila understood that the Master Code was no longer theory—it was their weapon.

Chapter 58: Lila Witnesses an Assassination Attempt

The streets were unusually quiet as Lila and her team left the council building, their minds racing from the successful infiltration. The rain had stopped, leaving puddles that reflected flickering lanterns.

"We did it," Jonah whispered, barely containing excitement. "The data... it's a goldmine."

Lila nodded, but her attention was elsewhere. Something in the shadows shifted—too deliberate to be a trick of the streetlights.

Suddenly, a sharp cry rang out from the far end of the alley. Lila spun, heart pounding. A council member was running, a folder clutched tightly against his chest. Behind him, a figure in black surged forward, a glint of steel catching the lantern light.

"Assassin!" Kira hissed, drawing her knife instinctively.

The team scattered into positions, blending into shadows, watching as the assassin lunged. The council member tripped, nearly dropping the folder. Lila's pulse raced—this was not just an attack; it was a message. Control maintained through fear and elimination.

Selene whispered, "We can't intervene directly—it's too risky. But we can record everything. Observe patterns, note weaknesses."

Lila's mind raced. Using the Master Code, she identified micro-movements in the assassin's stance, the council member's reactions, and nearby enforcer patrols. Every detail was crucial.

The assassin struck again, but this time, Lila signaled silently to Jonah. He nudged a loose crate into the path of the attacker, buying precious seconds. The council member scrambled to his feet, escaping into the mist.

Lila exhaled sharply. "They're sending a warning. Obedience, fear, loyalty—every action enforces control. But now we have insight. Every pattern, every weakness... we can map it."

Elias placed a hand on her shoulder. "This is the cost of knowledge. Observation saves lives without taking them, but the risk is real. We must tread carefully."

As the fog swallowed the alley, Lila's resolve strengthened. The organization's enforcers were ruthless, but with the Master Code, careful planning, and strategic observation, survival and resistance were possible.

She looked at her team. "We're not just surviving. We're learning. And one day, we strike back."

Chapter 59: Organization's Enforcers Tighten Control

The town felt heavier that morning, as if the very air carried the weight of fear. Doors were bolted, shutters closed, and citizens moved with careful precision, heads down, voices hushed. Lila noticed subtle changes immediately—the enforcers had increased patrols, and minor obedience rules were being enforced with ruthless efficiency.

Elias scanned the street with a practiced eye. "They know something happened last night. The council member barely escaped. The organization is responding, tightening control."

Kira's jaw clenched. "So everyone's terrified now. Even minor infractions are punished. We're running out of space to maneuver."

Lila observed patterns of movement, noting enforcer rotations, curfew compliance, and citizen behavior under surveillance. "They're reinforcing fear systematically," she said quietly. "Every patrol, every punishment, every whisper of warning strengthens obedience. But... patterns are predictable if you know what to look for."

Jonah frowned. "Predictable? Are we talking about using the Master Code to manipulate them again?"

"Yes," Lila said firmly. "Observation is key. If we understand the rules they reinforce and the way they enforce them, we can find vulnerabilities. Every enforcer, every minor law, every citizen reaction—these are pieces of a larger puzzle."

Samir glanced nervously at the increased patrols. "But with so much tightening, one mistake... and we're exposed."

"That's why we move carefully," Elias said. "We test responses, record patterns, and strike indirectly. Direct confrontation isn't an option yet. This is about preparation and information."

Lila's gaze swept the streets. Each citizen's compliance, each enforcer's action, every subtle adjustment—the organization's control was absolute, yet fragile in its predictability. With careful strategy, the same rules that oppressed the town could now be used to their advantage.

"We'll adapt," Lila said, determination hardening her voice. "We learn, we observe, and we plan. Fear is their weapon—but knowledge is ours."

The enforcers' shadows stretched across the cobblestones, and Lila felt the weight of the challenge ahead. Every tightened rule, every fearful citizen, and every enforcer was now a piece of the strategy she had to master. Survival wasn't enough—she had to think, act, and anticipate like the organization itself.

Chapter 60: Learning Manipulation Tactics on Townspeople (Advanced)

The town square buzzed with quiet activity, the early morning fog softening the sharp edges of the cobblestones. Lila and her allies positioned themselves strategically, observing citizens who moved with careful compliance. Every step, every glance, every gesture was weighed against the omnipresent threat of the organization's enforcers.

Selene crouched beside Lila, whispering, "This is where subtlety becomes power. Fear has limits. Observation, suggestion, and strategic nudges—that's how you influence behavior without drawing attention."

Lila nodded, eyes scanning the crowd. "Minor obedience rules, amplified through observation... but what's next? How do we test influence without exposure?"

Elias pointed to a young baker arranging bread in his window. "See him? He complies, yes. But he also reacts predictably to small cues. Shift his routine subtly—watch for hesitation or compliance. That's where you begin manipulation."

Lila carefully signaled the baker to rearrange a display, a minor adjustment in line with the patterns she had mapped using the Master Code. The baker paused, then continued exactly as expected. Every micro-behavior confirmed her calculations.

Kira whispered, "It feels... strange. Like we're puppeteers."

"Knowledge is responsibility," Lila said softly. "We aren't harming anyone—yet—but we're learning how obedience can be influenced. Every citizen, every enforcer, every minor law—it's data. Patterns, predictability, leverage."

Jonah observed a shopkeeper subtly following a new pedestrian rule. "So, tiny nudges build understanding. Not control yet—but insight?"

"Exactly," Lila confirmed. "Insight allows prediction. Prediction allows strategy. If we make one mistake, exposure could be deadly. But careful manipulation, combined with ethics, is how the Master Code becomes actionable."

As fog lifted, Lila realized that the town was both an enemy and a laboratory. Every citizen's reaction, every subtle enforcement, every hidden gaze—these were pieces of the system she was learning to decode. And every lesson she applied brought her closer to **undermining the organization from within**.

By dusk, Lila and her allies had mapped dozens of interactions, minor patterns, and small behavioral deviations. The Master Code was no longer abstract—it was alive, a living network of cause and effect, ready to guide her next moves.

Chapter 61: Planning a Major Operation to Expose the Organization

The greenhouse felt alive with tension. Lanterns flickered against damp walls as Lila spread the gathered files across the table. Maps, coded notes, and surveillance reports littered the surface. Selene stood behind her, whispering instructions while Elias and Jonah reviewed patrol patterns. Kira and Samir exchanged wary glances.

"This is it," Lila said, her voice steady but heavy. "Everything we've learned—the Master Code, the hidden networks, the obedience patterns—they all lead here. We plan carefully, or we risk everything."

Selene nodded. "The operation must be surgical. We expose enough to destabilize their hierarchy, but avoid immediate retaliation that could decimate civilians."

Jonah frowned. "Are you sure we're ready? Last time we acted subtly. This is... overt. It's dangerous."

"It has to happen," Lila said firmly. "The organization's grip is suffocating. If we do nothing, they'll tighten it further. Every citizen, every ally—more lives will be lost. We've observed their weaknesses long enough. Now we act strategically."

Elias tapped a point on the map. "Their surveillance nodes are concentrated here and here. If we can redirect attention, exploit gaps, and use coded messages, we can reach critical council files. That's our target."

Kira muttered, "And the enforcers?"

"They'll react," Lila admitted. "But we have the Master Code. If we predict their responses, manipulate minor obedience patterns, and coordinate with resistance contacts, we increase the odds of success."

Samir swallowed hard. "And if it fails?"

Lila met his gaze. "Failure has consequences. But inaction guarantees control continues unchallenged. Every small act we've practiced prepares us for this. Timing, observation, strategy, ethics—all of it converges here."

The team nodded solemnly. Outside, the town remained unaware that rebellion was brewing beneath the surface. And for the first time, Lila truly felt the weight of leadership—the lives of friends, citizens, and herself balanced precariously on the edge of a single, calculated plan.

Chapter 62: Discovering Hidden Weaknesses in Their System

The greenhouse was quieter than usual, the team spread across maps, notes, and the faint glow of Selene's tablet. Every enforcer movement, patrol schedule, and obedience pattern they had recorded was laid out like a chessboard.

Lila traced her finger over a series of interconnected nodes representing surveillance points. "The Master Code isn't just a blueprint—it's a machine," she said softly. "Every enforcer, every minor rule, every loyalty check feeds the network. But machines have weak points. We just have to find them."

Elias leaned closer. "Look at these rotation patterns. Certain intersections are predictable—five-minute windows where enforcers are absent, just enough time to move undetected."

Jonah frowned. "And the citizens? Any deviation could expose us."

"Exactly," Lila said. "We can't manipulate people directly yet. But the system itself has flaws—overloaded nodes, redundant communications, enforcement blind spots. That's where we start. Exploit the system, not the people."

Selene added, "Also notice the obedience micro-rules. Some are inconsistent, enforced unevenly. People trained to follow every minor law falter under contradictory signals. That's another vulnerability."

Kira's eyes narrowed. "So we trigger small contradictions... subtly, without anyone noticing?"

"Yes," Lila confirmed. "Disrupt patterns, create hesitation, and exploit gaps in communication. The organization relies on predictability. We turn that against them."

Samir hesitated. "And if they catch on?"

"They will," Lila admitted. "But the point isn't perfection—it's strategic disruption. Even small weaknesses, if applied correctly, create leverage. That's how revolutions start—not by strength alone, but by exploiting cracks in the armor."

The team worked through the night, identifying minor enforcement flaws, overlooked digital trails, and behavioral inconsistencies. Every weakness they cataloged became a potential foothold for the rebellion, a thread they could pull to unravel control.

By dawn, Lila felt a mixture of anticipation and dread. They had discovered vulnerabilities, yes—but they also realized how fragile their operation would be. Every decision, every move, every application of the Master Code would have to be precise. One misstep, and the organization would retaliate with lethal force.

Chapter 63: Lila is Captured but Manages Subtle Resistance

The alley was silent, but Lila sensed it before she saw it—a flicker of movement at the corner of her eye. Before she could react, a net of shadowed figures lunged, wrapping her in ropes and dragging her into the darkness.

"Lila!" Jonah shouted from a nearby rooftop, but she had already disappeared from view.

The room she was thrown into was stark, illuminated by a single overhead light. Enforcers stood at attention, their masks concealing expressions, their posture rigid. A figure emerged from the shadows—a council enforcer, one Lila had never seen up close.

"You've been curious," he said, voice low, controlled. "Curiosity is dangerous."

Lila's pulse raced, but she kept her composure. "I'm just observing," she said softly, testing tone, expression, and posture—the subtle cues she had practiced countless times.

The enforcer circled her, scrutinizing. "Observation alone can be fatal. Do you understand the consequences of defiance?"

"Yes," she replied. But inwardly, she began activating subtle resistance strategies. Tiny shifts in eye contact, micro-gestures, and calculated pauses—a silent message to anyone watching or listening. If she could manipulate perception, even slightly, it might buy her time.

Hours passed in tense silence. Lila learned to read their patterns: the rhythm of their steps, the cadence of their voices, the timing of their attention. She discovered that even in control, the enforcers had blind spots. A flick of a finger, a glance, a slight hesitation—they revealed uncertainty.

Selene's coded message had prepared her for this: *Observe. Wait. Influence without exposure.* She tested a subtle manipulation, planting doubt in the enforcer's mind through contradictory statements and careful phrasing. A flicker of hesitation. Success.

By nightfall, Lila found an opportunity. A minor lapse in surveillance—a delayed footstep, a distracted guard—allowed her to slip a hidden pin from her sleeve and unlock the restraints. As quietly as she could, she exited, leaving the enforcers unaware she had been manipulating them from the start.

Outside, the rain had returned, soft and relentless. Lila's breath steadied. She had survived, but the encounter left her shaken. Observation, patience, and the Master Code had saved her—but every encounter now carried higher stakes.

She knew one truth with certainty: **resistance required cunning, not strength alone, and even small acts could undermine the organization from within.**

Chapter 64: First Major Loss: A Close Ally is Killed

The night air was thick with tension as Lila and her team moved cautiously through the outskirts of town. Every shadow felt like a potential threat, every distant footstep a harbinger of danger. They were returning from a small operation—testing patterns of minor obedience rules—when the attack came.

A sudden explosion tore through the alley ahead, throwing Lila off balance. Dust and debris filled the air, and the team scattered instinctively. Shouts echoed as enforcers emerged from the mist, their faces hidden behind masks.

"Kira!" Jonah shouted, sprinting toward her as she lay pinned beneath a fallen beam. Lila's heart froze.

Selene moved quickly, trying to lift the debris, but Lila saw the realization dawn in her eyes: Kira wouldn't get up. A single, precise strike had pierced her chest beneath the armor of her vest—a methodical, execution-like attack.

"No..." Lila whispered, gripping the edge of the beam. Her mind raced, replaying every moment leading up to the attack. They had been careful, using the Master Code to avoid detection—but the organization had anticipated their movements.

Elias knelt beside Kira, checking for signs of life. "She's gone," he said quietly. "We weren't fast enough."

Samir sank to the ground, face pale. "It's... it's my fault. I should have—"

Lila shook her head, tears brimming but her voice steady. "No. The organization planned this. It wasn't anyone's fault. But we survive, we observe, and we use what she gave us to fight smarter. That's what Kira would have wanted."

Selene's hand rested on Lila's shoulder. "Every operation carries risk. Every victory has a cost. But her death isn't in vain. We learn, adapt, and keep going."

Lila closed her eyes for a moment, feeling the weight of leadership and loss. The Master Code wasn't just about strategy—it was about decision-making under impossible conditions, about surviving ethically and continuing the mission despite the cost.

The team gathered Kira's belongings and moved silently into the shadows, grief tempered by resolve. Every loss sharpened their focus, every sacrifice a reminder: rebellion carried consequences, and survival depended on cunning, courage, and the careful application of knowledge.

Chapter 65: Escaping with Secret Files

The night was thick with smoke and rain as Lila and her remaining allies regrouped. The alley where Kira had fallen was littered with debris, the air heavy with the acrid scent of fear and burning wood. Every shadow seemed to twitch with enforcer eyes, watching, waiting.

Lila's hand gripped the small satchel she had slung over her shoulder. Inside were the secret files they had risked everything to obtain—maps, coded communications, surveillance patterns, and fragments of council intelligence. These were the seeds of rebellion, but now they felt more fragile than ever.

"Move quickly," Selene whispered, glancing toward the perimeter where enforcers had begun searching. "We can't linger."

Jonah's hands shook slightly as he adjusted the satchel strap. "I can't believe Kira... she—"

"She sacrificed so we could survive," Lila interrupted gently, voice firm. "And we honor that by completing this mission. We escape, we preserve the files, and we continue. That's how her death has purpose."

They slipped through narrow alleyways, every movement calculated, every step aligned with the Master Code's predictive patterns. Lila's mind raced—she monitored patrol rotations, minor behavioral cues, and even the distant flicker of lanterns as signals of enforcer shifts.

A sudden creak of wood behind them sent a jolt of adrenaline through her veins. Lila froze, subtly adjusting her posture and gaze. An enforcer passed without noticing them, moving along a predictable path exactly as she had calculated.

Finally, they reached a hidden entry into the underground resistance network—a narrow tunnel beneath a deserted bakery. Heart pounding, Lila slipped the files into a secure locker and double-checked the encryption mechanisms Selene had devised.

"These files are the lifeline of the next phase," Selene said, eyes scanning the shadows. "Without them, we cannot plan the larger operation."

Lila nodded, determination replacing grief. "We survived tonight, not by luck, but by observation, strategy, and the Master Code. Every risk we take, every life lost, teaches us how to fight smarter. Now we have the information. Now we plan."

Outside, the town slept under the organization's tightening control, unaware that rebellion had just grown stronger in its hidden corridors. And for the first time since Kira's death, Lila felt the spark of hope that knowledge—and courage—could turn the tide.

Chapter 66: Underground Resistance Network Forms

The hidden chamber beneath the abandoned bakery was alive with whispered conversations and flickering lanterns. Maps, files, and coded messages were spread across tables, connecting locations, enforcer rotations, and citizen behavior into a web of intelligence. Lila stood at the center, observing the energy, the urgency, and the raw determination of the people around her.

Selene stepped forward, her eyes scanning the room. "We've gathered contacts from across the town—and beyond. Farmers, shopkeepers, messengers, even some former minor enforcers. Each understands the risks and has agreed to act subtly. This is the core of the resistance."

Jonah frowned. "That's a lot of people. How do we coordinate without getting caught?"

"Signals, coded messages, and observation," Lila replied, tracing her finger over the maps. "Each cell operates independently, but we share intelligence and patterns. The Master Code allows us to predict enforcer movements, so we can guide actions without exposing the network."

Samir looked uneasy. "And if the organization discovers any one of them?"

"That's why it's decentralized," Lila explained. "We don't rely on any single person. Failure in one area doesn't compromise the entire network. Each cell knows its role, its vulnerabilities, and its blind spots."

Elias added, "It's a balance of risk and reward. Each act of minor rebellion, each subtle manipulation, strengthens the overall strategy. The organization believes obedience is absolute—but distributed knowledge and calculated resistance can outmaneuver control."

Lila paused, looking around the room at the determined faces. "This network is more than a tool—it's a statement. We are learning, adapting, and resisting. Every piece of intelligence we've gathered, every pattern we've observed, and every minor rule we've bent brings us closer to weakening their hold. We fight not with brute force, but with precision, strategy, and conscience."

Selene handed Lila a small envelope of encrypted messages. "These are from other cells outside the town. They've been waiting for coordination. We can synchronize small operations, test influence, and map enforcement patterns on a larger scale."

Lila smiled faintly, a flicker of hope igniting despite the weight of losses. "Then we begin. Every connection we form, every ally we protect, every action we take moves us closer to the goal. The organization may tighten control, but the resistance is alive—and growing."

Outside, the night pressed against the walls of the bakery, but inside, the room pulsed with quiet defiance. Lila felt the full weight of responsibility settle on her shoulders, yet for the first time since Kira's death, she felt ready. The rebellion had a heartbeat—and she would lead it.

Chapter 67: Organization Retaliates Against Her Community

The morning fog clung to the town like a suffocating blanket. Smoke spiraled from the outskirts where small fires had erupted, and the distant sounds of alarms and shouts echoed through the narrow streets. Lila's heart pounded as she and the team hurried through hidden alleys, guided by Selene's surveillance notes.

"They know," Selene said quietly, her face pale. "The organization knows we've formed a resistance. This is retaliation."

Jonah clenched his fists. "They're punishing the town? Innocent people?"

Lila's jaw tightened. "Yes. And that's why we need to act smart. We can't stop them all at once—but we can limit damage and create diversions."

They reached the square just as enforcers moved systematically, enforcing curfews and terrorizing anyone caught outside. Citizens cowered, whispering pleas for mercy as the patrols executed their "obedience reinforcement" with ruthless efficiency.

Elias scanned the scene. "Every retaliation is predictable. We can anticipate their pattern—shift attention, guide enforcers away from vulnerable areas, and protect the most critical targets."

Lila took a deep breath. She focused on the Master Code principles: observation, prediction, influence. Small nudges, subtle diversions, and whispered warnings—each calculated move helped citizens avoid punishment without drawing attention.

A merchant froze as an enforcer approached, threatening punishment for leaving shutters open. Lila signaled discreetly, causing a minor distraction by tossing a pebble to redirect the patrol. The merchant slipped inside, unharmed.

Selene leaned closer. "This is it. Real-world application of the Code—ethics, survival, influence—all in motion."

By nightfall, the team had mitigated some of the worst retaliation but not all. Smoke hung over the town like a grim reminder: rebellion came at a price. Innocent lives had been affected, and the organization's ruthlessness had grown clearer.

Lila's resolve hardened. "Every action we take now must be precise. We can't allow fear to control the town, but we must protect as many lives as possible while striking at their weaknesses. This is the cost of rebellion—and we have to live with it."

Outside the bakery, the underground network regrouped. The town was bruised but not broken. And for Lila, every retaliation strengthened her determination: the organization could punish, but it could not yet stop the resistance.

Chapter 68: Public Exposure Attempt Fails

The town square had been meticulously chosen. Lila stood atop the steps of the abandoned courthouse, files and evidence of the organization's manipulations tucked securely in her satchel. Citizens gathered cautiously, curiosity mingling with fear. The team was hidden among the crowd, ready to support and intervene if necessary.

"This is it," Lila whispered to Selene. "Everything we've learned—the Master Code, surveillance data, citizen patterns—it all comes down to this moment."

Jonah fidgeted nervously beside her. "Do you think they'll listen? Or are we just exposing ourselves?"

"We have to try," Lila said firmly. She raised her voice, projecting conviction. "People of the town! The organization that controls us enforces obedience through fear and secrecy. The laws you follow blindly are manipulated to maintain power over your lives!"

A murmur ran through the crowd. Faces shifted uneasily. A few whispered in agreement, but most froze, hesitant to act. Lila signaled subtly, trying to engage those she had observed as receptive, but the ripple of influence barely spread.

Suddenly, masked enforcers appeared at the edges of the square, moving swiftly to block exits and isolate her team. The crowd scattered in fear, some citizens fleeing, others retreating to safety. The rebellion attempt had been anticipated.

Selene hissed, tugging Lila to the side. "They knew we would try this. It was a trap."

Elias helped Lila retreat through a hidden alley. "Exposure can work," he said grimly, "but timing, strategy, and subtle influence are everything. Public confrontation under surveillance was too risky."

Lila's shoulders sagged with frustration. The plan had failed, but she refused to let despair take hold. "We learn from this," she said through gritted teeth. "We adapt. The Master Code isn't about bold gestures—it's about precision, understanding, and striking when the system is weakest."

Jonah scowled. "It felt like we were shouting into the wind."

"Then we whisper next time," Lila said, eyes burning with resolve. "Every citizen is a node, every pattern is exploitable, and every small success counts. One failure does not define us—it teaches us."

As the rain began to drizzle over the cobblestones, Lila felt the weight of responsibility settle heavier than ever. The organization's grip was tighter, their surveillance more acute—but knowledge, strategy, and perseverance were still in her hands.

Chapter 69: Allies Start Doubting Her Leadership

The underground chamber was unusually quiet. Lila sat at the center table, fingers tracing the edges of maps and files, trying to process the failed exposure attempt. Around her, the team's energy was taut with frustration and unease.

Jonah broke the silence first. "I have to say it... Lila, I don't know if this is working. Every time we try something bold, we risk lives—and last night nearly cost us everything."

Selene leaned back, arms crossed. "He's not wrong. The public exposure failed, and now the organization knows we're moving openly. We've been lucky so far."

Elias adjusted his glasses, frowning. "Leadership isn't just about courage—it's about judgment. Sometimes restraint is better than action. We need to reconsider tactics."

Lila's chest tightened. "I understand your concerns," she said carefully, keeping her tone measured. "Every move we make carries risk, but inaction allows the organization to tighten control further. We've observed, analyzed, and learned patterns. We adapt. That's the strategy."

Samir shifted nervously. "It feels like we're gambling with everyone's lives. Are you sure we're ready for this?"

"I've never been more certain," Lila replied firmly, though a flicker of doubt gnawed at her. "I may not have all the answers, but we've survived every close call, exploited every weakness, and learned more than the organization expects. We are building the resistance, and we need unity, not hesitation."

Kira's absence hung in the room like a shadow, a silent reminder of the cost of leadership. Jonah's gaze softened, but he remained unconvinced. "We'll follow you," he said finally, "but we need to be sure that every plan is airtight. No more exposure attempts without preparation."

Selene nodded. "Agreed. Lila, your instincts are good, but strategy must guide us more than bold gestures. The Master Code is a tool—let's apply it rigorously."

Lila exhaled slowly, absorbing the tension. Leadership was no longer just about daring acts—it was about careful balance, strategic foresight, and earning the trust of those depending on her. Failure wasn't an option—not just for herself, but for the lives intertwined with their rebellion.

"I hear you," Lila said, standing. "We regroup, refine plans, and proceed with precision. The organization may doubt our capabilities, but we will not falter. Every decision now carries weight, and we'll wield it wisely."

The team nodded, renewed focus blending with cautious determination. Doubt lingered—but so did loyalty, and for Lila, the challenge of leading was clearer than ever.

Chapter 70: Lila Uncovers Her Father's Involvement with the Organization

The underground chamber was quiet, but Lila's mind was anything but. Selene had handed her an envelope marked with a symbol she recognized from her father's old book—the Master Code emblem. The paper inside contained fragments of communications, coded meeting logs, and a photograph of her father shaking hands with a figure she immediately recognized as a senior council enforcer.

Her breath caught. "This... this changes everything," Lila whispered.

Jonah leaned over her shoulder. "Are you saying your father... worked with them?"

Lila's fingers trembled as she examined more documents: financial records, meeting minutes, and notes written in the same cryptic style as *The Obedience Code*. "He was more than an observer," she said softly. "He was involved in designing parts of their system—possibly even the laws of obedience themselves."

Selene's eyes were sharp. "This is dangerous information. It explains how the Master Code is so precise—and why you can interpret it so intuitively. But it also means betrayal runs deep, even in your family."

"I need to know why," Lila said, voice quivering. "Did he support them willingly? Or was he trying to manipulate from within?"

Elias adjusted his glasses. "We may never know the full answer. But what matters is what you do now. Knowledge of his involvement gives us insight—and leverage. You can anticipate patterns he may have created, gaps he may have left intentionally."

Lila stared at the photograph again. The man she had loved, the father she thought she understood, was now a figure intertwined with the very organization she had vowed to fight. Her heart pounded, a mixture of grief, anger, and determination.

“This isn’t a reason to quit,” she said finally, looking at her team. “It’s a reason to be smarter. If my father helped build the system, then we know its architecture. Every weakness, every loophole, every pattern—it’s a roadmap we can use.”

Selene placed a hand on her shoulder. “We follow your lead, Lila. Your father’s choices don’t define you. The Master Code gives us guidance—we decide how to wield it.”

Lila exhaled, resolving the turmoil in her chest. The revelation was painful, but it strengthened her purpose. The rebellion was no longer just a fight against the organization—it was a mission to reclaim the integrity stolen from her family and her town.

Chapter 71: Secret Messages Lead to Hidden Archives

The dim light of the underground chamber flickered against walls lined with maps, files, and cryptic symbols. Lila spread the newly discovered messages across the table, her eyes scanning patterns that only someone familiar with her father's handwriting could recognize. Each symbol, each coded line, hinted at locations beyond the town—places that had remained hidden for decades.

Selene leaned in, whispering, "These aren't just old communications—they're instructions. Your father left breadcrumbs to secret archives. But only someone trained in the Master Code could decipher them."

Lila's fingers traced a series of interlocking symbols. "He wanted me to find these," she murmured. "Not just as a puzzle... as preparation. These archives may contain the organization's original blueprints—their vulnerabilities, operational strategies, and even the Master Code's deepest secrets."

Jonah frowned. "So all this time, the answers were hidden from everyone—except you?"

"Yes," Lila said, a mix of awe and dread in her voice. "If I'm right, these archives could give us leverage to challenge the organization. But they're heavily guarded—physically and through coded security protocols. Any misstep could alert the enforcers immediately."

Elias adjusted his glasses, scanning the decrypted instructions. "The paths described here are precise. Timing, observation, and subtle obedience cues are embedded. It's a test—and a roadmap."

Selene's voice was soft but firm. "We need to be meticulous. Every step, every symbol, every pattern must be followed exactly. The organization's reach is extensive, but knowledge is power. And this... this could be the turning point."

Lila felt a surge of determination. Her father's shadow hung over the discovery, complicated and fraught with moral ambiguity—but the potential was undeniable. Hidden archives could expose the organization's weaknesses, provide strategic intelligence, and maybe even reveal a way to dismantle control from the inside.

"Then we move," Lila said decisively. "We follow the messages, uncover the archives, and learn everything we can. The Master Code isn't just about obedience anymore—it's our path to rebellion."

As the team prepared for the journey, every mind focused, every hand steady, the weight of responsibility pressed down on Lila. One false move could destroy lives—but the right move could shift the balance of power forever.

Chapter 72: Lila Learns the Master Code Can Override Loyalty

The hidden archives were a cavern of whispers and shadows, walls lined with ancient tomes, coded manuscripts, and neatly stacked files detailing decades of the organization's operations. Lila carefully lifted a thick volume from a shelf, her fingers brushing the embossed title: *The Obedience Code: Extended Directives.*

Selene peered over her shoulder. "This is deeper than your father's personal notes. These instructions explain not only obedience but how to influence loyalty itself."

Lila's heart quickened. "Influence loyalty? You mean... bend someone's allegiance without them realizing it?"

"Yes," Selene said, eyes scanning the pages. "Through the Master Code, certain obedience patterns can be applied to override conditioned loyalty. It's psychological architecture—subtle cues, timed reinforcement, strategic contradictions. Used ethically, it can protect citizens. Used recklessly, it can turn allies into tools of the organization."

Jonah leaned closer, frowning. "So you're saying we could theoretically change someone's allegiance—either to us or... to them?"

Lila nodded, flipping through diagrams showing micro-behaviors, reinforcement schedules, and coded communication loops. "This is powerful. It explains how the organization maintains control over enforcers and civilians alike. And it's why the Master Code is more than predictive—it's directive. Carefully applied, it allows influence without overt coercion."

Selene's voice was solemn. "It's a tool—and a moral test. Every action has consequences. Overriding loyalty without consent walks a fine line between protection and manipulation."

Lila inhaled, absorbing the weight of the revelation. "If we can use this strategically, we could neutralize threats, strengthen the resistance, and even turn enforcers against the organization. But it requires precision, patience, and ethics. One mistake, one misapplied pattern, and we could lose everything—or worse, betray our own principles."

Elias added cautiously, "This gives us leverage but demands restraint. The Master Code isn't just survival—it's the architecture of trust and influence. Misuse could make us indistinguishable from the organization we fight."

Lila closed the book, determination shining in her eyes. "We use it wisely. To protect, to save lives, to dismantle control—but never to dominate. The organization may have weaponized obedience, but we will weaponize knowledge and conscience."

As the team absorbed the implications, Lila felt the full weight of responsibility settle upon her shoulders. The Master Code was no longer just a guide—it was a tool that could change the course of rebellion, but only if wielded with care, morality, and unyielding focus.

Chapter 73: Plan to Use Master Code in Rebellion

The underground chamber was alive with focused energy. Maps, encrypted messages, and diagrams of behavioral patterns sprawled across tables as Lila and her team gathered around. The discovery of the Master Code's power to influence loyalty had changed the stakes—and the strategy.

"We can't just react anymore," Lila said, tracing lines on the map that indicated enforcer patrols, communication hubs, and vulnerable nodes. "We need a plan that targets the organization at its structural core, using the Master Code to shift allegiance subtly. Influence, not force. Observation, not chaos."

Selene nodded. "We've identified enforcers and minor officials who follow loyalty patterns rigidly. If we introduce precise contradictions and timed obedience cues, we can create hesitation, doubt, and eventually, compliance toward our cause."

Jonah's brow furrowed. "So we manipulate them? That sounds... risky. And morally gray."

"Yes," Lila admitted. "It is. But we'll only use the Master Code where absolutely necessary—on those whose actions directly endanger civilians or our network. Precision, subtlety, and ethics guide every move. Our goal isn't domination—it's dismantling control."

Elias chimed in, "We'll need a multi-stage plan: small tests first, then coordinated influence, and finally leveraging allies who've been convinced through pattern reinforcement. Each step has to be measured. Missteps could expose the network."

Lila glanced at the team. "We practice, we rehearse, we test minor obedience rules in controlled scenarios. Then we escalate gradually. Every action documented, every influence observed. This is strategic rebellion. This is how we use knowledge to fight without causing unnecessary harm."

Selene added, "The key is synchronization. We can't act alone. Each cell must understand the timing, the cues, and the signals. The Master Code gives us leverage—but only if we act collectively, consistently, and ethically."

Jonah sighed, nodding reluctantly. "It's a lot to coordinate... but if it works, we could really shake the organization from the inside."

Lila's gaze hardened. "We don't have a choice. The organization's grip tightens every day. This plan, executed with precision, is our path to weakening them, protecting civilians, and reclaiming freedom. The Master Code is our tool—but ethics, courage, and intelligence will wield it."

The team began outlining their first series of coordinated actions, each movement, signal, and timing calculated with painstaking care. Outside, the night pressed against the hidden chamber, but inside, the resistance pulsed with purpose, knowledge, and resolve. For the first time, rebellion felt tangible—and winnable.

Chapter 74: Organization Identifies Lila as Top Threat

The underground chamber was tense, the air thick with the quiet hum of whispers and strategy. Lila scanned the encrypted messages Selene had just decrypted. Her stomach sank as the meaning became clear.

"They know," Selene said softly, eyes wide. "They've identified you as the primary threat—the one who understands the Master Code, anticipates their patterns, and coordinates the resistance."

Jonah froze. "So it's personal now. They're coming for you... for us."

Lila's jaw tightened. "Not just coming—they'll use everything in their arsenal to eliminate me. But we've prepared for this. Observation, prediction, influence. The Master Code isn't just defensive—it's strategic."

Elias adjusted his glasses, scanning the files. "They're reorganizing patrols, tightening surveillance, and planting potential informants. Every predictable behavior we've relied on is being altered. They're adapting."

Selene's voice was grim. "Which means we have to act faster, smarter, and more subtly. Any public exposure attempts or large movements will be trapped. This is a time for precision, stealth, and calculated influence."

Lila exhaled slowly, absorbing the gravity of the moment. "We've always been careful, but now everything is heightened. One wrong move, one missed cue, and they could dismantle the network—or worse."

Jonah's tone was sharp. "And if they capture you? We can't just hide underground forever."

Lila's eyes hardened. "Then we ensure that capture is impossible. The Master Code teaches us to anticipate patterns, create blind spots, and manipulate perceived obedience. We'll stay two steps ahead, and if they overreach, they'll expose themselves."

Selene handed Lila a small, coded map. "These are their new movements and surveillance zones. Study it carefully. Every pattern you see is a clue. Every weakness we find now can be leveraged to stay alive and protect the resistance."

Lila nodded, determination burning brighter than fear. "They may have marked me, but knowledge is power. We move strategically, influence subtly, and strike at vulnerabilities only we understand. They may see me as the top threat—but we will turn that perception against them."

As the team leaned over the maps, the storm outside mirrored the tension within. The organization had identified the threat—but Lila was ready to lead, adapt, and survive. The rebellion had entered its most dangerous phase yet, and every decision would shape not only her fate but the future of the town and the underground network she had built.

Chapter 75: Narrow Escape from Assassination Attempt

The streets were slick with rain, the fog thick enough to blur the outlines of buildings and lanterns. Lila moved cautiously, satchel of secret files secured tightly against her side. Selene and Jonah flanked her, eyes scanning every shadow, every flicker of movement.

"They've increased patrols," Selene whispered. "They know you're the top threat. Stay alert."

Lila nodded, heart pounding. She felt the weight of every decision, every prediction, every calculated risk. The Master Code had taught her to anticipate behaviors—but some variables were unpredictable.

A sudden clang echoed from a nearby alley. Lila froze. Before she could react, a masked figure lunged from the shadows, a blade glinting under the dim lantern light.

"Move!" Jonah shouted, pulling her to the side. The attacker's strike grazed her shoulder, sending a shock of pain through her body.

Selene acted instantly, throwing a small smoke device she had concealed. The dense cloud filled the alley, masking their movements and confusing the assailant. Lila pressed herself against a wall, using her awareness of the environment to plan the next step.

"They're counting on panic," she muttered. "We stay calm, observe, influence their perception."

Using a combination of timing, movement, and minor misdirection—the subtle cues of the Master Code—Lila guided the attacker's attention away, ducking behind barrels and slipping into a narrow side street. Jonah followed, keeping watch for reinforcements.

Minutes felt like hours as they navigated the fog-shrouded streets, every step measured. Finally, they reached a safe house prearranged for emergencies. Lila sank to the floor, breathing heavily but alive.

Selene placed a hand on her shoulder. "You applied the Master Code perfectly. Observation, timing, and influence—it saved your life."

Lila exhaled slowly, wincing at the pain in her shoulder. "It's not just about survival anymore. Every encounter teaches us—how they think, how they react, and where their blind spots are. We adapt, and we keep moving."

Jonah's voice was grim but determined. "They'll come again. And next time, it might not be just one assassin."

Lila's eyes hardened. "Then we'll be ready. Every threat is an opportunity to learn, every attack a clue. They've marked me as a top threat, but that only makes me more dangerous to them."

Outside, the fog rolled on, hiding the streets and the enemies within them. Inside the safe house, Lila and her team prepared, knowing that every narrow escape strengthened their strategy, sharpened their focus, and pushed the rebellion closer to its turning point.

Chapter 76: Coordinating with Scattered Resistance Cells

The safe house hummed with quiet activity. Maps, encrypted messages, and diagrams littered the tables. Lila stood at the center, reviewing the latest intelligence from Selene: updates from resistance cells in nearby districts, coded signals, and reports on minor enforcer patrols.

"We need to synchronize operations across all cells," Lila said, pointing to the maps. "The organization is tightening control, but if we act collectively, we can exploit their blind spots."

Jonah frowned. "How do we ensure communication without being detected? Last time, the organization adapted quickly to any disruption."

Selene tapped a series of symbols on a tablet. "Encrypted messages, time-delayed signals, and pattern-based cues. Each cell operates independently but reacts to the same triggers. The Master Code helps predict enforcer responses, so each action remains subtle yet effective."

Elias adjusted his glasses. "We also need contingency plans. Some cells might be compromised, and we can't risk a single failure cascading across the network."

Lila nodded. "Exactly. Each node must be self-sufficient, yet coordinated. If one is exposed, others remain intact. Observation, adaptation, and influence will guide every move."

Selene added, "We'll start small—minor obedience manipulations, subtle diversions, and influence tests. Each success will provide real-time intelligence and confidence for larger operations."

Jonah shook his head. "It's a lot of variables. One wrong step could collapse the network."

"Then we adapt," Lila said firmly. "The Master Code isn't just prediction—it's strategy. We monitor, we adjust, and we act when timing is perfect. Every pattern we identify gives us leverage. Every coordinated step makes the organization react, rather than control us."

As the team plotted their first series of synchronized actions, Lila felt a renewed sense of purpose. The rebellion was no longer isolated—it was a living, adaptive network, growing stronger with every careful move.

Outside, the night was quiet, but the network pulsed with unseen life. Messages traveled through coded signals, citizens subtly influenced, and enforcers unknowingly nudged toward distraction. The Master Code guided each step, transforming scattered cells into a coordinated force.

Lila glanced at her team. "We're no longer just surviving. We're shaping the battlefield. The organization may see me as a top threat, but together, we are unstoppable."

Chapter 77: Betrayal Shakes the Team

The underground chamber felt heavier than usual, as if the walls themselves carried tension. Lila scanned the latest reports from the scattered resistance cells, her stomach tightening. Something was wrong—patterns didn't align, signals had been intercepted, and one of their most reliable contacts had gone silent.

Selene broke the silence. "Lila... we've been compromised. Someone on the inside has been feeding information to the organization."

Jonah's face went pale. "What? Who would do that? We've been so careful."

Lila shook her head slowly, trying to control the rising panic. "I don't know yet. But we can't let this stop us. We need to identify the traitor before more lives are endangered. Observation, deduction, and careful interrogation—everything the Master Code teaches us—will be essential."

Elias furrowed his brow. "It could be one of the newer members. Someone we trusted implicitly. We need to act fast before they sabotage the entire network."

Selene handed Lila a small, coded message intercepted from the organization. "This was clearly written with knowledge only someone in the inner circle would have. It contains details about last night's diversion—details no outsider could know."

Lila clenched her fists. "Then the betrayal runs deep. But we can turn it into an advantage. By identifying the mole, we can feed false information and manipulate the organization's response. Every action becomes a lesson, every misstep a clue."

Jonah's voice was tense. "I trusted them. How can we trust anyone now?"

"You trust the network," Lila said firmly, meeting his gaze. "Trust is distributed, not personal. One betrayal won't destroy us if the Master

Code guides our decisions. Observe patterns, test loyalty subtly, and ensure redundancy in every cell. The organization thrives on fear—we thrive on knowledge and strategy."

Selene nodded. "We'll set traps, monitor reactions, and reveal the mole without exposing the entire network. Precision is key."

Lila exhaled, determination blazing. "Betrayal is painful, but it doesn't stop the rebellion. It sharpens us. It teaches us to act smarter, anticipate weaknesses, and stay one step ahead. We will find the traitor—and we will survive stronger."

Outside, the storm raged, mirroring the turmoil within. Inside, Lila and her team prepared, aware that every decision could save lives—or cost them. The rebellion was tested, but resilience and strategy would ensure it endured.

Chapter 78: Lila's Moral Compass Challenged: Innocent Lives at Risk

The rain fell in relentless sheets outside the hidden safe house, drumming against the metal roof as Lila studied the latest intelligence reports. Enforcer activity had intensified, and civilians caught in minor rebellions were being punished. Some of the scattered cells had reported casualties—innocent lives caught in the crossfire of resistance efforts.

Selene looked up from a coded map. "We have a dilemma. A cell has been discovered, and the organization is threatening to execute hostages if we don't comply with a minor obedience directive."

Jonah's face paled. "We can't just obey them... can we?"

Lila swallowed hard, her mind racing. "If we obey, we save lives, but we reinforce their control. If we resist, we risk execution—but we weaken the organization strategically."

Elias spoke cautiously. "The Master Code allows us to influence indirectly, but we have to act with precision. Every wrong signal could cost more lives."

Lila clenched her fists, recalling her father's notes. *The code is power, but power without conscience is destruction.* "We can't act recklessly. We have to find a way to protect the innocents without giving the organization the victory."

Selene leaned closer. "There's a minor obedience loophole—one that allows the hostages to escape if we manipulate the enforcers' timing and focus. But it's risky, and it requires exact coordination."

Lila's jaw tightened. "Then that's our path. Every step must be calculated. Observation, subtle cues, and influence—nothing more, nothing less. No one dies if we execute this correctly."

As the team prepared, Lila felt the heavy weight of moral responsibility pressing on her. Every decision now was a test: her skills, her ethics, and her ability to prioritize human life over immediate rebellion gains.

The operation began at dusk. Using coded signals, misdirection, and precise timing, Lila orchestrated the escape. Heart pounding, she watched as the hostages slipped past enforcers, their fear slowly turning to relief.

When the dust settled, Selene whispered, "You did it. No lives lost, and the organization doesn't realize the manipulation."

Lila exhaled slowly, a mix of relief and lingering guilt in her chest. "This is the reality of rebellion. Every choice matters. Every life matters. And sometimes, morality and strategy must coexist—even when the path is razor-thin."

Outside, the storm cleared, leaving the night eerily quiet. Inside, Lila's resolve hardened. The Master Code was not just a tool for strategy—it was a guide for conscience, even in the most dangerous circumstances.

Chapter 79: Act 3 Climax: Organization Closes In, Rebellion Seems Doomed

The underground network buzzed with unease. Every encrypted signal, every minor diversion, every coded message pointed to the same terrifying conclusion: the organization was closing in. Surveillance drones hovered closer, enforcer patrols had multiplied, and loyal informants had infiltrated previously secure cells.

Lila paced, the weight of leadership pressing heavily on her shoulders. "They know exactly where we are," she murmured, tracing maps with her finger. "Every pattern, every loophole we exploited—they've adapted. We're running out of time."

Jonah's voice trembled. "We've always been careful, but now... it feels like they're unstoppable. How do we fight an enemy that anticipates every move?"

Selene leaned over the table, pointing to the network diagrams. "We leverage unpredictability. The Master Code teaches influence, but also adaptation. Every enforcer, every informant, every citizen has a predictable behavior pattern—but only if we act as expected. We break their expectations."

Elias nodded. "We can create decoys, manipulate perception, and force the organization into reactive positions. But the margin for error is razor-thin. One misstep, and the entire rebellion collapses."

Lila's eyes narrowed. "Then we act precisely. Coordinated signals, minor obedience manipulations, and controlled diversions. Every action must maximize confusion for them, while protecting our cells."

A sudden alarm echoed—a drone had spotted a movement in one of the inner chambers. Lila's heart raced. "It's begun. They've cut off some escape routes. We need to implement contingency plans, now."

Selene handed her a series of coded instructions. "These will guide the cells through misdirection and safe extraction. Follow strictly. Any deviation risks everything."

Lila inhaled deeply. "Then we execute. For every life, for every citizen, for every cell. We fight not with brute force, but with intelligence, influence, and the Master Code. They may close in, but they underestimate our adaptability—and that is their vulnerability."

The team moved with synchronized precision, each action, signal, and diversion calculated to perfection. The streets outside became a maze of controlled chaos, the organization reacting, but never fully anticipating the resistance's subtle maneuvers.

For a fleeting moment, it seemed as if the rebellion might crumble entirely—but Lila's strategic use of knowledge, timing, and influence kept hope alive. The fight was far from over—but for the first time, the organization realized that the resistance was not merely surviving—it was learning, adapting, and striking back in ways they had never predicted.

Chapter 80: High-Stakes Conflicts, Strategic Sabotage, and Incremental Victories

The city streets were alive with tension. The organization's enforcers patrolled with precision, but subtle disturbances began to ripple through their ranks—small acts of sabotage coordinated by Lila and her scattered resistance cells.

Selene whispered over a secure line, "The minor obedience manipulations are working. Enforcer patrols are being delayed, communications misdirected. They're reacting, not controlling."

Jonah's eyes widened as he watched a convoy of supplies derail under carefully timed diversions. "They didn't see this coming... and neither did the informants embedded in their network."

Lila's mind raced. "Every conflict, every sabotage must maximize impact while minimizing civilian risk. The Master Code guides us. Influence behavior patterns, create controlled chaos, and force adaptation on the organization."

Elias adjusted the decrypted maps. "Cells report successful extractions of files, and enforcers are beginning to question internal loyalty. Subtle influence is spreading. We're creating cracks."

Selene smiled faintly. "Incremental victories are our momentum. They may have thought the resistance was broken, but each success compounds. Doubt will grow, fear will spread, and their predictable patterns will work against them."

Lila leaned over the table, determination burning in her eyes. "We coordinate diversions with intelligence gathering. Every action has two purposes: disrupt the organization and strengthen the resistance. Every success is data for the next strike."

Jonah clenched his fists. "It feels surreal... like we're winning by outthinking them instead of confronting them head-on."

"That's the point," Lila said firmly. "Force is predictable. Influence is invisible. And knowledge—the Master Code—is unstoppable if applied correctly."

As night fell, the resistance continued its subtle sabotage, every move precise, every action calculated. Civilians remained mostly unaware, but their small acts of obedience and defiance subtly shifted the balance. The organization, powerful and ruthless, was learning too late that Lila's strategy had created an adaptive, intelligent, and morally grounded resistance.

For the first time, hope was tangible. Incremental victories, each meticulously planned and executed, began to turn the tide. The rebellion had survived near collapse and now had a fighting chance.

Chapter 81: Secrets of The Obedience Code Revealed; Lila Grows Into a Leader

The hidden archives had become a sanctuary of knowledge and strategy. Lila sifted through her father's meticulously coded writings, cross-referencing patterns, diagrams, and encrypted notes. The Master Code, once a tool for obedience, was now a lens through which she could understand the organization's inner workings.

Selene leaned over her shoulder. "These pages... they're more than just instructions. They reveal the hierarchy, the subtle psychological levers, and even the weaknesses built into the system. Your father left this intentionally, knowing someone would use it to challenge them."

Jonah frowned. "So all this time, we've been learning not just how to survive—but how to outthink them?"

"Yes," Lila said, tracing a series of diagrams illustrating influence networks and behavioral triggers. "The Obedience Code isn't just a book of rules—it's a blueprint for power. And understanding it fully gives us the ability to manipulate patterns ethically, protect civilians, and dismantle the organization from within."

Elias adjusted his glasses, scanning the newly decrypted sections. "Some of these entries indicate contingency protocols. The organization was aware that someone could eventually decode their system. Your father left failsafes—and that knowledge is now ours."

Selene's voice softened. "It's also why you've grown into a leader. You've learned to balance intelligence, morality, and courage—qualities the organization underestimates."

Lila exhaled slowly, absorbing the weight of the revelation. "Every mission, every risk, every betrayal... it's led to this. The Master Code isn't just strategy—it's insight into human behavior, loyalty, and ethics. We can protect, influence, and dismantle, but only if we act wisely."

Jonah's eyes brightened with renewed confidence. "We've come a long way—from scattered cells to a coordinated resistance. And you... you've become the leader we needed."

Lila's gaze hardened, determination blazing. "Leadership isn't about titles—it's about responsibility, sacrifice, and vision. We've survived attacks, betrayal, and moral dilemmas. Now we use what we've learned, not just to survive—but to reclaim control from those who manipulate obedience for power."

The team nodded, united and focused. Outside, the city lay cloaked in shadows, but inside the chamber, the rebellion pulsed with knowledge, strategy, and a leader transformed by understanding. The Obedience Code, once a symbol of control, had become a weapon of insight—and Lila's growth from student to leader was complete.

Chapter 82: Lila and Team Prepare for Final Confrontation

The safe house was alive with activity, but tension hung heavy in the air. Every corner was mapped, every escape route noted, every contingency drilled. Lila stood at the center, reviewing the final intelligence reports with Selene, Jonah, and Elias. The organization was tightening its grip, but the resistance had grown stronger, smarter, and more coordinated.

"We've identified their core operations hubs," Lila said, pointing to the maps. "The enforcers' response patterns, communications nodes, and minor council chambers—they're all predictable if we apply the Master Code strategically."

Selene nodded. "It's all about timing and influence. Subtle diversions, obedience manipulations, and psychological triggers can destabilize their command structure without unnecessary casualties. But one misstep could be catastrophic."

Jonah clenched his fists. "We've faced near-death situations before, but this... this feels different. It's the culmination of everything we've learned."

Lila's eyes hardened. "It is. But we've also learned, observed, and adapted. Every incremental victory, every lesson from betrayal, every ethical choice—it's brought us here. We know their weaknesses, we understand patterns, and we can act collectively."

Elias added cautiously, "We also need backup plans for every scenario—safe extractions, fallback cells, and coded communication protocols. The Master Code is powerful, but it isn't infallible."

Lila took a deep breath. "We move in unison, with precision. Every cell knows their role. Every action serves multiple purposes: destabilize the organization, protect civilians, and gather intelligence for the final strike. Timing, influence, and ethical judgment guide us. We do not underestimate them, but we do not fear them either."

Selene placed a hand on Lila's shoulder. "You've become a leader worthy of this fight. We follow your plan, your timing, and your decisions."

Lila exhaled slowly, feeling the weight of responsibility but also the clarity of purpose. "Tonight, we take the next step. The organization believes it controls obedience, but we control knowledge, strategy, and morality. Every move will bring us closer to ending their grip. We strike not with chaos, but with precision, and we emerge with the future in our hands."

Outside, the city slept under the cover of night, unaware of the calculated storm about to be unleashed. Inside, the team prepared, every mind focused, every step rehearsed. The final confrontation was imminent—and Lila was ready to lead the rebellion into history.

Chapter 83: The Final Infiltration Begins

Night had fallen, casting the city in shadows. Lila and her team moved silently through alleyways, rooftops, and underground passages, every step measured, every signal precise. The organization's hubs—once thought impenetrable—were within reach, but the risk was immense.

"This is it," Lila whispered, crouching behind a low wall. "All cells are in position. Timing must be perfect. Every distraction, every minor obedience manipulation, every signal has to align."

Selene adjusted her earpiece. "I've synchronized communications. Any deviation triggers immediate backup protocols. Observation is key—react, don't act rashly."

Jonah's eyes scanned the streets. "They've increased patrols at every entrance. One misstep and we're exposed."

Lila nodded, recalling her father's teachings. *Predict patterns, exploit obedience, but always prioritize ethics.* She activated a small device, sending subtle cues to distract the nearest patrols—nudging them into predictable loops while keeping civilians safe.

"Enforcer movement patterns are adapting," Selene murmured. "They're noticing the manipulations, but it's subtle enough—they think it's coincidence."

"Exactly," Lila said. "We stay calm, influence behavior without aggression, and move through their blind spots. Remember, the Master Code isn't just a strategy—it's our shield."

As the team advanced, Lila's heart pounded, adrenaline sharpening her focus. Every corridor, every room, every hallway had been mapped in the codes and signals derived from the Obedience Code. They moved as one—silent, precise, and coordinated.

Suddenly, a faint sound echoed from above. Lila froze, signaling for Jonah and Selene to halt. Shadows shifted in the corridor ahead—an enforcer patrol approaching. She activated a minor obedience cue—a subtle pattern in their behavior learned from previous manipulations—and the enforcers paused, hesitated, and moved past, unaware of the team's presence.

Selene exhaled quietly. "Perfect execution. They didn't see a thing."

Lila allowed herself a brief nod. "This is how we reclaim control. One step at a time, calculated, ethical, and unstoppable."

As they pressed deeper into the heart of the organization's operations, Lila felt the culmination of all her training, observation, and moral decisions guiding her. The final infiltration had begun—and the rebellion's success depended on every subtle influence, every ethical choice, and every precise action executed perfectly.

Chapter 84: Turning the Organization's Patterns Against Them

The deeper Lila and her team ventured into the organization's headquarters, the more their plan relied on subtle influence and strategic misdirection. Every corridor, surveillance camera, and enforcer patrol had predictable patterns, and Lila intended to use those patterns against them.

"Observation first," Lila whispered, crouching behind a steel support beam. "Every enforcer has routines. Every schedule has a flaw. We exploit timing, not force. Influence, don't attack."

Selene nodded, tapping into a handheld device that analyzed enforcer movements. "They're highly trained, but predictable. Minor obedience loops, previously implanted via civilians and lower-ranked enforcers, create small delays. We amplify them strategically."

Jonah's eyes narrowed. "So we let them move, but manipulate their perception so they act exactly how we need?"

"Exactly," Lila said, scanning the main control room ahead. "We'll trigger micro-cues—signals only detectable subconsciously by those trained under the organization's obedience rules. They'll hesitate, question themselves, and react in ways that open paths for us."

Elias adjusted the final schematic. "We can redirect security patrols without them realizing it, creating blind spots in critical areas. The organization is brilliant at control, but rigid patterns make them exploitable."

Lila's mind raced, implementing the plan step by step. Every light flicker, every door alarm, every minor interruption was calculated to bend the enforcers' reactions while keeping civilians safe.

Selene whispered, "It's working. Patrols are off schedule, communication loops are feeding back incorrect data, and internal confusion is growing."

Lila allowed herself a brief, controlled smile. "We've learned their code. Now we use it against them. Influence over obedience. Prediction over force. Knowledge over fear."

As the team moved through corridors, past distracted enforcers, and toward the organization's central control, Lila felt a surge of confidence. The patterns the organization relied upon for dominance were now the very tools of its undoing. Every hesitation, every flawed reaction, was a victory.

By the time they reached the heart of the headquarters, Lila's team was invisible, precise, and fully synchronized. The organization, for all its power, had become a predictable system—and predictability was now their vulnerability.

Chapter 85: First Major Sabotage Inside the Organization

The control hub of the organization loomed ahead, a labyrinth of glass panels, digital monitors, and humming servers. Lila crouched just outside the central chamber, her pulse steady but her mind alert. Every member of her team knew their role, every action timed to the second.

"This is it," Lila whispered. "Our first major sabotage. If executed perfectly, it will disrupt communication, delay enforcers, and create critical confusion throughout the organization."

Selene tapped her tablet, eyes scanning the schematics. "Security cameras looped. Doors and sensors temporarily disabled. Minor obedience cues planted in nearby enforcers. They won't notice until the disruption spreads."

Jonah glanced at the locked main console. "And what about the central systems? That's where everything—communications, schedules, reports—intersects."

Lila's lips tightened. "We're going to hit it at the core. The Master Code allows us to predict reactions. The instant we trigger the overload, confusion spreads. Enforcers hesitate. Patterns break. Control fractures—but only for a short window. We move fast, precise, ethical."

Elias's hands moved quickly over the interface, overriding security protocols while Selene manipulated surveillance feeds. "We're live. Once I trigger this, the patterns cascade. Minor obedience triggers will amplify the effect."

Lila inhaled deeply. "Three... two... one..." She pressed the activation key.

Immediately, alarms flashed across monitors. Lights flickered. Internal communications loops scrambled. Enforcers hesitated, unsure whether to follow orders or investigate anomalies. The carefully timed obedience cues spread confusion, causing minor breakdowns in movement and response across the headquarters.

Selene whispered with a triumphant smile, "It's working. They're reacting exactly as predicted. Delays, miscommunications… it's perfect."

Jonah exhaled sharply. "This is incredible. We've turned their control system against them."

Lila scanned the room, her gaze steady. "One step at a time. We sabotage, we influence, we extract critical intelligence. No civilians harmed, no unnecessary risk. That's how we win—through knowledge, precision, and ethical action."

By the time the alarms subsided, the organization was disoriented, communication lines fractured, and enforcers hesitant in their movements. Lila's team had struck a decisive blow without bloodshed, demonstrating the power of calculated influence and the Master Code's strategic application.

The rebellion's momentum surged. One major sabotage had shaken the foundations of control, giving hope and leverage to the resistance—and setting the stage for the next critical steps in dismantling the organization.

Chapter 86: Exposing the Master Code's Full Potential

The control hub still hummed with fragmented signals, monitors flickering like broken mirrors. Lila and her team moved deeper into the heart of the organization, each step guided by the knowledge they had painstakingly pieced together from her father's Obedience Code.

"This is it," Lila whispered, scanning the mainframe. "Every minor sabotage, every influence cue we've planted—it all leads here. If we apply the Master Code fully, we can destabilize their operations and manipulate their hierarchy from the inside."

Selene adjusted the encrypted interface. "We can trigger cascading loops in their obedience protocols. Enforcers will hesitate, internal communications will misfire, and their decision-making will become reactive, not proactive."

Jonah swallowed hard. "So we're not just attacking their systems—we're influencing their minds, making them act predictably while we remain invisible?"

"Exactly," Lila replied. "But we do it ethically. No unnecessary harm, no civilian casualties. The Master Code is about understanding patterns, predicting behavior, and controlling outcomes without violence whenever possible."

Elias inserted the final override. "Cascading loops ready. Once activated, their command structure will fracture temporarily, giving us access to their central intelligence, personnel files, and operational blueprints."

Lila's fingers hovered over the activation key. "Three things to remember: influence, observation, and timing. Execute perfectly, and we gain not just control—but insight."

She pressed the key. Immediately, screens flickered, doors misaligned, and enforcers paused mid-action, hesitating as pre-programmed obedience patterns faltered. Minor directives conflicted, schedules collided, and internal protocols broke down.

Selene's eyes sparkled. "It's magnificent. Every enforcer is reacting to their own confusion. We're ghosts in their system."

Lila exhaled, surveying the room. "The Master Code isn't just a guide for obedience—it's a map of influence. Every movement, every choice, every reaction can be predicted and guided if you understand the rules. And now... we can use that knowledge to dismantle them, step by step."

As files streamed into their secure devices, Lila realized the full power of the Obedience Code. Not just survival, not just subtle influence—but transformation. Knowledge and ethical application had become weapons. The organization had created control through obedience, but Lila would reclaim freedom through understanding—and precision.

The team shared a silent nod. The rebellion was no longer just reactive. It was strategic, informed, and unstoppable.

Chapter 87: Infiltrating the Inner Council

The inner chambers of the organization were unlike anything Lila had seen. Polished floors reflected the harsh overhead lights, while walls were lined with monitors displaying every operation, every cell, every minor movement. This was the nerve center—the Inner Council itself.

Selene whispered, crouching behind a console. "This is where decisions are made. Every policy, every punishment, every strategic move originates here. One wrong step and we're exposed immediately."

Jonah swallowed hard. "And these people... they're ruthless. Trained to manipulate, enforce, and eliminate anyone who resists."

Lila's eyes narrowed. "Which is why subtlety is key. Observation first. Influence second. And timing... timing above all." She scanned the room, noting guards, cameras, and the council members themselves. Each had predictable behavioral patterns, adherence to protocol, and obedience loops the Master Code could exploit.

Elias tapped his tablet, overlaying a simulated distraction route. "If we activate these minor obedience cues, we can guide the guards away, delay council response, and move through the room unnoticed."

Selene adjusted her earpiece. "Civilians have been cleared from the area. Only council members and enforcers remain. Any resistance must be handled without raising alarms."

Lila inhaled, recalling her father's final notes. *Power is structure, but structure is predictable. Observe, influence, and bend patterns subtly, and you hold control.*

Step by step, the team advanced. Minor lights flickered in the council room, subtle signals caused guards to hesitate, and Lila's team slipped past surveillance blind spots. Every action mirrored obedience cues embedded in previous operations, turning the council's own protocols into obstacles against them.

Finally, Lila and her closest allies reached the central chamber. Council members turned, surprised but slow to react, their obedience loops temporarily disrupted. Lila stepped forward, voice calm but firm.

"This ends tonight," she said, her tone carrying the authority she had earned through every decision, every moral dilemma, and every calculated risk. "We know your rules, your manipulations, and your secrets. The Obedience Code is no longer yours—it belongs to those who choose freedom, strategy, and ethics over blind compliance."

A tense silence filled the room. Lila knew this moment marked the turning point. The Inner Council, for all their power, now faced the consequence of their own predictable structure—and the rebellion's strength, guided by knowledge and moral clarity, was ready to dismantle it.

Chapter 88: Exposing the Council's Secrets

The Inner Council room trembled with tension. Lila stood at its center, her team strategically positioned around her. Monitors flickered, displaying the organization's operations, as council members attempted to assess the sudden disruption.

Selene whispered, "They're trying to regain composure, but the obedience loops we manipulated earlier are causing hesitation. Every decision is delayed—exactly as predicted."

Lila took a deep breath. "It's time to reveal what they've tried to hide for decades." She tapped her tablet, sending encrypted files and decoded evidence from the Obedience Code to every monitor in the room. Names of informants, records of manipulated civilians, financial corruption, and secret punishments flashed across screens.

Jonah's jaw dropped. "They didn't anticipate transparency. This... this will crumble their authority instantly."

The council members reacted with shock, fear, and confusion. Commands collided with obedience cues gone awry, creating chaos in decision-making. Each secret exposed undermined their credibility, revealing not strength but manipulation, exploitation, and fear-driven control.

Lila's voice rang out, firm and unwavering. "You built a system on obedience, fear, and secrecy. But secrecy is fragile. Knowledge is power—and we now hold it. Your influence over people's lives is finished. The Obedience Code guides strategy, yes—but it also guides conscience. And your conscience has been revealed to the world."

Selene added, "Every council member, every enforcer, and every manipulated civilian will now see the truth. Patterns you relied on to control behavior are collapsing."

Elias's fingers moved quickly, ensuring copies of the files reached secure channels outside the headquarters. "The public and resistance cells now have indisputable evidence. Your control is no longer absolute. Every predictable reaction will now work against you."

The council members glared at Lila, but their authority was hollow. Fear had replaced obedience, and hesitation had replaced action. With their secrets exposed, the organization's internal power structure was fractured beyond repair.

Lila stepped forward, calm and resolute. "Your rules dictated obedience. But knowledge dictates freedom. And today, freedom wins."

Outside the chamber, subtle signals rippled through the city. The rebellion's coordinated efforts, grounded in the Master Code and ethical strategy, were bearing fruit. The organization's once-unshakable control was unraveling—and Lila's leadership had turned the tide.

Chapter 89: Coordinating the Collapse

The Inner Council was reeling from the exposure of their secrets. Lila and her team moved quickly, understanding that hesitation could allow the organization to regroup. Every moment was critical, and the Master Code guided their every decision.

Selene tapped into the building's network. "We can synchronize the cells now. Every faction, every operative, every safe house can act simultaneously. The organization won't know what hit them."

Jonah glanced nervously at the monitors. "So we collapse them from all sides at once? Total coordination?"

Lila nodded firmly. "Yes. But precision is essential. We dismantle infrastructure, disrupt communications, and influence obedience loops—all without endangering civilians. Every move is calculated, every signal intentional."

Elias checked the timing protocols. "The minor sabotages we planted earlier will cascade perfectly with this final push. Enforcers will be overextended, commands will conflict, and internal panic will spread."

Selene adjusted her earpiece. "We're ready. Cells outside are standing by. Once we signal, every node will act in unison."

Lila exhaled, feeling the weight of leadership. "Remember, we act ethically. Influence patterns, redirect forces, and neutralize threats without unnecessary harm. The organization thrives on fear and obedience. Today, we turn their tools against them."

With a subtle nod, Lila activated the first signal. Across the city, resistance cells sprang into action. Surveillance loops scrambled. Supply lines were disrupted. Internal communications faltered. The enforcers' obedience patterns conflicted, creating chaos and uncertainty.

Selene's voice crackled through the earpiece. "It's working. Every cell executing perfectly. The organization is unraveling."

Jonah grinned. "It's like watching a web collapse from the center outward."

Lila's eyes narrowed, focused. "This is the culmination of every lesson, every betrayal, every strategy we've implemented. Knowledge, ethical influence, and precise timing—this is how we dismantle an empire built on obedience."

By the end of the night, the organization's infrastructure was fractured, leadership confused, and enforcers immobilized by conflicting directives. The collapse was coordinated, efficient, and calculated. Lila's rebellion had struck at the very heart of power—and the Master Code had guided them to victory.

Chapter 90: Act 3 Climax and Aftermath

Dawn broke over the city, soft light spilling across streets that had once been dominated by fear and control. Lila stood at the center of the safe house, exhausted but resolute, as the final signals from the coordinated collapse reached every resistance cell. The organization's command infrastructure was paralyzed, enforcers frozen by conflicting obedience loops, and the Inner Council powerless to regain control.

Selene exhaled slowly. "It's over... at least for now. They can't regroup immediately. The rebellion has won the first—and most decisive—battle."

Jonah shook his head, awe in his eyes. "I can't believe it. The city... it feels alive again. Free."

Lila's gaze lingered on the monitors showing empty council chambers and deactivated systems. "Freedom is fragile. Control is subtle. But knowledge, precision, and ethics can dismantle even the strongest systems. We've proved that today."

Elias stepped forward. "The Master Code... it guided every decision. Every sabotage, every manipulation, every ethical dilemma—it worked because we understood the rules and applied them responsibly."

Selene smiled faintly. "And you... you've grown into a leader who embodies all of it. Strategy, morality, courage. You didn't just survive—you taught others how to act, think, and resist."

Lila exhaled, a mix of relief and reflection washing over her. "This rebellion isn't just about destroying control—it's about creating a system where people understand the rules, choose to act ethically, and learn to influence with responsibility. That's the true power of the Obedience Code."

Outside, the city stirred. Citizens cautiously returned to streets once ruled by fear. Resistance cells worked to restore order and ensure that the organization's collapse didn't leave chaos in its wake. Lila's team moved among them, guiding, protecting, and teaching.

For the first time in years, obedience was voluntary, knowledge was power, and freedom was tangible. The rebellion had survived near collapse, adapted, and emerged victorious. But Lila knew this was only the beginning. Control might resurface in new forms, and challenges would arise—but with the Obedience Code as a guide and her team united, she was ready to face whatever came next.

The city was free, the organization fractured, and Lila had proven that understanding, courage, and ethics could outmatch even the most powerful systems. The Obedience Code had been reclaimed—and this victory, hard-won and precise, was just the first step toward a future built on conscious choice rather than blind obedience.

Chapter 91: The Organization Strikes Back

The night was unnervingly still. From their safe house, Lila and her team watched the city through a web of monitors, scanning for any sign of movement. For weeks, the organization had been fractured and paralyzed, but now whispers indicated it was regrouping.

Selene's voice broke the silence. "I'm picking up multiple anomalies in their minor hubs. They're consolidating forces and preparing a counterstrike. Timing looks immediate."

Jonah clenched his fists. "So after all we've done, they're coming for us one last time?"

Lila's eyes narrowed, determination flashing. "They think we're reacting. But we've learned their patterns. We can predict their moves, and we can turn their obedience loops against them."

Elias adjusted the holographic map projected above the table. "Their enforcers are converging on the north sector. Civilians are still in the area. Any frontal assault risks too many lives."

Lila exhaled and activated a digital overlay. "We don't attack blindly. We create subtle disruptions, distractions in their behavior, and misdirect their forces. Minor obedience cues, pattern prediction... the Master Code guides every step."

Selene studied the projections. "If we apply the cues correctly, their patrols will hesitate, and we can manipulate their hierarchy remotely. It's risky—but feasible."

Jonah's jaw tightened. "What about surprises? Leader-level enforcers?"

"Predicted reactions," Lila replied firmly. "We've anticipated contingencies. Every enforcer has a predictable loop. We exploit hesitation, misdirection, and knowledge. Collateral damage must be zero, civilians protected, but control of the sector must shift to us."

Hours passed in tense preparation. Lila coordinated each cell via encrypted signals, timing disruptions down to the second. Every movement, every minor cue, every observation was meticulously calculated.

Then the first signals triggered. Enforcers hesitated mid-stride. Patrols collided, repeated commands faltered. Confusion rippled outward, subtle yet devastating. Lila watched intently, her pulse steady.

"Pattern disruption successful," Selene whispered. "They don't know what's happening. They think it's coincidence."

Lila allowed herself a brief, controlled smile. "Coincidence is a luxury they lost long ago. Knowledge and ethical influence will guide this city through its final battle for freedom."

Outside, the city trembled with unseen movements. The organization was striking back—but Lila had already anticipated every step. The counterattack had begun, but for the first time, it played into the rebellion's hands.

Chapter 92: Leader Unveiled

The safe house buzzed with tension. Lila's monitors tracked every movement of the organization's regrouping forces, but her mind was focused on one question: who was truly behind the remnants of control?

Selene's voice cut through the silence. "I've intercepted communications. They're consolidating under a single command structure. Whoever is leading this... it's personal."

Jonah frowned. "Personal? You mean... someone with a connection to us?"

Lila's heart skipped. Memories of her father and the Obedience Code swirled in her mind. "Possibly. We've seen fragments, but nothing conclusive. Whoever it is, they know the rules we use. They know our patterns."

Minutes later, encrypted footage arrived. Lila's breath caught. On the screen stood a figure tall and imposing, eyes sharp and calculating. The leader's face was partially obscured, but something familiar tugged at Lila's memory.

Selene leaned closer. "Recognition confirmed. The figure matches files we recovered from your father's notes. Lila... it's him—your father's former partner, the one who disappeared years ago. The one you never understood."

Jonah's eyes widened. "Wait... he's alive? And leading this? That's... insane."

Lila clenched her fists. "Not just alive. He's orchestrating every move. This isn't just an organization—it's personal. Everything my father worked on, every lesson in the Obedience Code, has been twisted and applied here."

Elias tapped the tablet nervously. "Their enforcers are following his exact behavioral loops. He's applying a Master Code of his own. And he's predicting our moves."

Lila's mind raced. "We have to anticipate him, not just the organization. Every tactic we've prepared will need adjustment. We face not only strategy but personal stakes—and we can't let emotions cloud judgment."

Selene exhaled. "This changes everything. It's not just rebellion anymore. It's a battle against someone who understands the Obedience Code as deeply as you do."

Lila stared at the screen, determination hardening. "Then we match knowledge with ethics. Precision with conscience. He may know the rules, but I know the consequences of misuse. And I will use that understanding to stop him—without sacrificing what we've built or the people we protect."

Outside, the city stirred, unaware of the confrontation brewing at its core. The organization's true leader had been revealed. And for the first time, Lila realized the rebellion was not just a fight for freedom—it was a confrontation with the legacy of power, obedience, and betrayal itself.

Chapter 93: Rallying the Allies

The safe house buzzed with urgency. Monitors displayed fragmented signals from scattered resistance cells across the city. Lila stood at the center, her team gathered around, all eyes fixed on her.

"This is it," Lila began, voice steady but commanding. "The organization has regrouped, and their leader is not just powerful—they know the Obedience Code. But knowledge is only dangerous if it's misused. We will use it responsibly, and we will coordinate every move to protect civilians while striking strategically."

Selene tapped her tablet, pulling up maps of the city and resistance cells. "We can synchronize all remaining teams, create overlapping zones of influence, and disrupt their obedience patterns simultaneously. Timing is critical—every second counts."

Jonah looked uneasy. "We've lost people before. Some of our best allies are gone. Are we ready for this?"

Lila's eyes softened but remained firm. "We remember those we've lost, and we honor them through precision and care. Every decision now is about protecting lives and dismantling control. We act ethically, strategically, and decisively. No reckless heroics. No unnecessary casualties."

Elias joined in, overlaying predicted responses of the organization's enforcers. "If we apply minor obedience cues across multiple nodes, we can misdirect them, isolate key leaders, and create hesitation. The leader will be forced to react to our moves instead of commanding theirs."

Selene nodded. "We also need to manage trust carefully. Some cells may have infiltrators. Communication will be encrypted and need verification at every step."

Lila took a deep breath. "Then we begin. Rally the allies. Confirm their positions. Activate the first wave of influence. Remember, our strength is knowledge, ethics, and coordination. The city is counting on us."

Minutes later, encrypted signals flashed across the city. Resistance cells moved with precision, implementing Lila's strategy. Patrols hesitated under subtly manipulated obedience loops, supply lines faltered, and communications conflicted. Lila monitored each action, adjusting cues in real time, her mind a web of strategy, ethics, and prediction.

Selene leaned close. "It's working. Hesitation, confusion, misalignmcnt... cxactly as wc prcdictcd."

Jonah grinned, tension easing slightly. "It's like watching the pieces fall into place, but all by design."

Lila's eyes burned with focus. "We act as one. Knowledge guides us, ethics steadies us, and courage drives us. This is the moment where the rebellion unites to face the final challenge."

Outside, the city prepared for a decisive confrontation. Allies were in position, civilians protected, and the organization's power structure vulnerable. For the first time, the rebellion had not only momentum—it had clarity, strategy, and the moral strength to win.

Chapter 94: The Master Code in Action

The city lay tense under a cold, dim light, streets quiet but filled with potential energy. Lila sat before a network of monitors, tablets, and encrypted feeds, her fingers dancing over keys as she coordinated the rebellion.

"This is it," Lila said, voice calm but resolute. "Every movement, every hesitation, every minor obedience cue is part of a larger pattern. We don't just fight—we guide."

Selene adjusted her earpiece. "The enforcers are reacting exactly as predicted. Hesitation, conflict between orders, misalignment of patrols... Lila, your timing is flawless."

Jonah leaned over her shoulder. "So we're manipulating their own obedience rules to make them fail? It's like turning their strength against them."

Lila nodded. "Exactly. Their system relies on absolute compliance. But predictability is their weakness. The Master Code lets us anticipate their reactions and influence outcomes ethically. We disrupt, we misdirect, and we neutralize—not with violence, but with understanding."

Elias pointed to a map overlay. "If we apply these loops simultaneously across multiple sectors, their command structure will fracture. Enforcers will hesitate, leaders will clash over decisions, and opportunities will open for resistance cells to act."

Selene's voice lowered, tense. "Some areas are high-risk. Collateral is minimal, but any miscalculation could endanger civilians."

Lila's eyes hardened. "Precision and ethics guide us. We avoid unnecessary harm. We act decisively, but responsibly. Every loop, every cue, every command we influence is a step toward dismantling control without sacrificing conscience."

Minutes turned into hours as the Master Code's influence rippled through the city. Patrols faltered, leadership commands conflicted, and enforcers questioned actions without realizing why. Resistance cells advanced strategically, civilians were protected, and Lila's team remained the unseen force guiding every outcome.

Jonah exhaled, awe in his voice. "It's working... like a perfectly orchestrated pattern."

Selene nodded. "Chaos, but guided. They can't adapt because every reaction is anticipated and influenced."

Lila leaned back, her gaze sharp and unwavering. "This is the power of knowledge and ethics combined. The Master Code isn't a weapon—it's understanding, prediction, and moral action. And with it, we reclaim freedom, step by step."

Outside, the organization's remnants floundered, their obedience-driven structure failing under its own rules. Lila's rebellion had turned their strength against them, and the final battle was no longer just a confrontation—it was a demonstration of precise, ethical control over chaos.

Chapter 95: Betrayal and Consequences

The tension in the safe house was palpable. Lila reviewed encrypted feeds from the resistance network, noting movements and responses, when a sudden alert froze her.

Selene's voice trembled slightly. "We have an anomaly in Sector 7. One of our cells... it's been compromised."

Jonah frowned. "Compromised? How? We verified all positions."

Lila's eyes narrowed. "Someone inside leaked information. Orders were followed, but signals were manipulated. We need to identify the traitor before more cells are exposed."

Minutes later, surveillance footage revealed the truth. A trusted operative, someone who had been with the rebellion since the earliest sabotage missions, was covertly transmitting data to the organization's remnants. The realization hit the team like a physical blow.

Selene whispered, voice tight with betrayal, "It's... it's Marik. I can't believe it. He was with us from the start."

Jonah's fists clenched. "How could he? After everything we've done?"

Lila inhaled sharply, steadying herself. "Emotions cannot cloud judgment now. We must act strategically and ethically. He's a threat, yes—but our priority is protecting the city and civilians. Retribution comes second."

Using the Master Code, Lila manipulated minor obedience cues to isolate Marik, predicting his reactions to minimize risk. The operative was cornered in a deserted warehouse, unable to call for reinforcements or endanger civilians.

Lila confronted him, calm but resolute. "Why, Marik? After everything, why betray us?"

Marik's face twisted with guilt and fear. "I... I thought I could survive by feeding them information. I didn't want to die. I didn't realize it would endanger everyone!"

"You chose obedience to fear over loyalty to freedom," Lila said. "Your actions endangered lives, but we stop here. You will face consequences, but ethically—no unnecessary harm."

Selene secured the operative while Jonah monitored outside for reinforcements. Marik was removed from the field, neutralized without fatality. The rebellion's integrity remained intact, though shaken.

Lila exhaled, her mind racing. "Betrayal is always a possibility. But strategy, ethics, and decisive action prevent it from destroying everything we've built. This is the cost of freedom and leadership."

Outside, the city continued to stir, oblivious to the internal struggle within the rebellion. Lila knew more challenges would come—but the lesson was clear: vigilance, trust, and moral clarity were as vital as strategy.

Chapter 96: Public Exposure

The city woke to an unusual quiet. Monitors across the safe house displayed live feeds from every corner, but today they weren't tracking enemy movements—they were broadcasting truth.

Lila stood before the central console, her fingers hovering over the activation sequence. "This is it. The people need to see what's been happening, not just here, but everywhere the organization has manipulated lives. Knowledge is power—and it's time to give it back."

Selene glanced at her nervously. "Are you sure? Once this goes public, there's no turning back. The chaos could be immediate."

Jonah crossed his arms. "It's a risk. But hiding it would only let them continue controlling people through fear."

Lila nodded. "We've protected civilians, ensured resistance cells are in place, and neutralized key enforcers. The city can absorb the truth—and it needs to. They deserve to know how deep the manipulation went."

Elias initiated the broadcast. Screens lit up across the city—public monitors, social networks, encrypted channels—all streaming documents, videos, and records from the Obedience Code revealing the organization's global manipulations. Names of informants, financial corruption, and psychological control tactics flashed, leaving nothing hidden.

Reactions were immediate. Crowds gathered, murmuring turned to shock, shock to outrage. Citizens who had long obeyed blindly now saw patterns, understood manipulation, and felt a surge of empowerment.

Selene whispered, awe in her voice, "They're... they're realizing it themselves. They see how they were controlled—and they're reacting responsibly."

Jonah smiled grimly. "No panic, no riots... yet. Just awareness. That's remarkable."

Lila exhaled, feeling a weight lift. "This is the power of ethical exposure. Knowledge, transparency, and conscience. The organization's authority is gone—not because we destroyed them physically, but because truth dismantled obedience."

Across the city, the ripple effect began. Enforcers hesitated, supporters questioned loyalty, and civilians discussed, debated, and chose consciously for the first time in years. The rebellion was no longer confined to a few cells—it had become a movement of awareness and empowerment.

Lila turned to her team. "We've taken the first step toward lasting change. The organization can no longer manipulate blindly. Its power exists only as long as ignorance does. And now, ignorance has ended."

The city breathed, unshackled at last, and Lila realized that the most potent weapon in their struggle had always been knowledge—shared openly, ethically, and courageously.

Chapter 97: Final Moral Test

The city was stirring under the first light of morning, the streets alive with whispers of truth and newfound awareness. Lila stood on the balcony of the safe house, gazing at the grid of activity below. The organization's remnants were scattered, their enforcers confused, their leadership fractured—but not entirely gone.

Selene joined her, voice low. "Reports indicate a last stronghold. Enforcers and a handful of leaders are hiding civilians as leverage. They're desperate."

Jonah grimaced. "So, what now? Storm in and risk lives? Or let them linger?"

Lila's hands clenched around the railing. "This is the final test—not of strength, but of conscience. We could strike and eliminate them entirely, ending the threat physically. Or we could use strategy, influence, and knowledge to neutralize their control ethically, sparing civilians even if it means some enemies survive."

Elias stepped forward. "The Master Code gives us options. Every loop, every obedience cue, every behavioral prediction... we can guide them without unnecessary bloodshed. But if we hesitate, they might regroup."

Lila closed her eyes, weighing morality against risk. Memories of friends lost, civilians endangered, and the lessons her father left behind swirled together. "Obedience without ethics is tyranny. Freedom without responsibility is chaos. We act with purpose and conscience. We neutralize their influence, not destroy human life unnecessarily."

Selene nodded, understanding. "We manipulate patterns, not people's lives. Influence outcomes, don't annihilate."

The team moved with precision. Subtle obedience cues disrupted the enforcers' decision loops. Conflicting commands caused hesitation.

Leaders argued among themselves, unable to act decisively. Civilians, guided by calm instructions from the resistance, were safely evacuated.

Jonah watched in awe. "It's... working. They can't regain control, but no one is hurt. Just... disoriented."

Lila exhaled, satisfaction tempered with fatigue. "This is the final moral test. Victory achieved without sacrificing ethics. We've dismantled control, empowered freedom, and upheld conscience. That is the true measure of leadership."

The organization's remnants collapsed under the weight of their own rules and Lila's ethical strategy. The city had survived not just a rebellion, but a triumph of conscience over blind obedience.

Chapter 98: Collapse of the Organization

The city's skyline shimmered in the morning light, but below the surface, chaos and confusion reigned among the remaining enforcers. Lila watched from the safe house, her team poised to act, every nerve tense yet controlled.

Selene's voice cut through the quiet. "All remaining enforcers are in disarray. Command structures have collapsed. The leaders are isolated and indecisive. Lila... it's now or never."

Jonah adjusted his gear, eyes scanning the monitors. "We can finish this, but we need to maintain control. Civilians are still at risk if we move too fast."

Lila nodded. "We dismantle them, not destroy them. The Master Code will guide their actions until they are neutralized. Every step, every hesitation we induce must prevent harm while stripping the organization of power."

Elias's fingers flew over his tablet. "Enforcers are splitting, some arguing among themselves, some surrendering. The patterns are exactly as predicted. Their own obedience loops are collapsing them from within."

Lila's heart pounded. "Then we apply the final sequence. Subtle disruptions, ethical guidance, and the Master Code applied across every remaining node. We end their influence permanently—but without needless violence."

Minutes passed, each more tense than the last. Slowly, enforcers dropped weapons, leaders surrendered, and communications ceased. Lila watched as the organization that had once ruled the city through fear and manipulation crumbled under its own structure and her team's calculated, ethical influence.

Selene exhaled, relief softening her features. "It's over. They can no longer harm anyone—or control anyone."

Jonah's voice was quiet, awed. "We did it... we actually did it."

Lila leaned back, letting the weight of the moment settle. "Not just through force or strategy, but through understanding, ethics, and careful guidance. The city is free, not because we destroyed them, but because we neutralized control responsibly. That is true power."

Outside, citizens cautiously emerged, witnessing the first truly autonomous day in years. The rebellion had succeeded. The organization had collapsed. And for the first time in decades, obedience was no longer blind—it was conscious, guided by awareness and choice.

Chapter 99: The Master Code's Future

The city was quiet now, almost eerily so. Streets that had once been patrolled by enforcers were now filled with cautious but free citizens. Lila walked through the safe house, the weight of recent events pressing on her, yet tempered by a deep sense of accomplishment.

Selene joined her, holding a stack of recovered manuscripts—the Obedience Code itself. "All copies are accounted for. Every file, every note, every iteration. Now the question is... what do we do with it?"

Lila ran her fingers over the worn pages of her father's original book. "Knowledge is power," she said slowly, "but it's also dangerous if misused. The organization turned obedience into a weapon. But the Master Code... it can guide, teach, and protect—if applied ethically."

Jonah leaned against the wall, thoughtful. "So... do we destroy it, hide it, or use it?"

"We preserve it," Lila replied firmly. "Not as a tool of control, but as a guide for understanding human behavior, ethical decision-making, and responsible leadership. It's a resource, not a weapon. It must never be used to dominate or coerce again."

Elias added, "We can teach future leaders, train resistance cells, and ensure the code is applied only to safeguard freedom, not enforce fear."

Lila nodded. "The Master Code belongs to those who value conscience over compliance, ethics over tyranny. Its lessons will guide the city, and perhaps the world, toward responsible decision-making and awareness. But access will be strictly controlled—wisdom with accountability."

Selene smiled softly. "So your father's legacy... it wasn't just the code. It was the responsibility to use knowledge wisely."

"Exactly," Lila said. "We've seen what happens when understanding is twisted. Now, we reclaim it for the right purpose. The Master Code will teach freedom, not fear."

Outside, the city thrived quietly, the first true day of autonomous choice since the organization's rise. Lila looked out over rooftops, alleyways, and streets filled with people making their own decisions.

She exhaled, a sense of calm washing over her. "The future is uncertain, as always. But knowledge, ethics, and choice—these are constants. And as long as we respect them, freedom will endure."

Chapter 100: Reflection and New Beginnings

The city hummed with quiet life, its citizens moving freely for the first time in years. Lila walked through the streets, her team beside her, observing people making choices, discussing, debating, and deciding for themselves. The weight of the rebellion, the betrayals, the victories, and losses rested heavily on her shoulders—but it was tempered by a deep sense of fulfillment.

Selene broke the silence. "Look at them. They're... thinking. Choosing. Not obeying blindly. It's... beautiful."

Lila smiled softly, her gaze sweeping the city she had fought to protect. "Freedom isn't the absence of rules—it's understanding why we follow them, and choosing responsibly. That's what we've given them. That's what the Master Code can teach."

Jonah nodded. "And we've survived, grown, and led ethically through it all. I never imagined we'd come this far."

Elias added, "The organization is gone, their enforcers disbanded, and knowledge has replaced fear. The city is safe... for now."

Lila paused, reflecting on her journey—from the discovery of her father's secret book to mastering the Obedience Code, confronting betrayal, and facing moral tests she never imagined. "We've learned the cost of obedience, the dangers of manipulation, and the power of ethical leadership. But most importantly, we've learned that conscience and knowledge together can overcome fear."

Selene touched her shoulder gently. "What now?"

Lila inhaled deeply. "Now, we rebuild—not just the city, but trust, community, and understanding. The Master Code will guide, but humans will choose. That is the future we fought for."

The sun rose higher, illuminating streets filled with life, laughter, and cautious hope. Citizens engaged in decisions once dictated by fear, now guided by awareness. Lila looked to the horizon, her heart steady.

"Obedience is no longer a chain," she said quietly, "but a choice. And with choice comes freedom."

For the first time in years, the city was not controlled. It was alive. It was free. And Lila—once a young girl discovering secrets in a hidden book—had become the leader who ensured that freedom endured.

Epilogue: Breaking Free

Months later, Lila walks through a freer society. Though shadows of the organization remain, she's established safeguards and networks to prevent abuse of power. The Obedience Code is no longer a tool of control—it's a lesson. Lila understands that true freedom requires vigilance, courage, and sometimes, breaking the rules. The story closes on a note of hope and cautious optimism, hinting at potential future challenges.

www.ingramcontent.com/pod-product-compliance
Lightning Source LLC
LaVergne TN
LVHW100308210926
848480LV00003B/1055